A CRADLE of THE REVOLUTION

VOICES *from* INYATHI SCHOOL

Matabeleland, Zimbabwe 1914-1980

edited by
Pathisa Nyathi
Marieke Clarke

A CRADLE OF THE REVOLUTION

VOICES FROM INYATHI SCHOOL, MATABELELAND, ZIMBABWE 1914-1980

ISBN 978-0-7974-9250-9
EAN 9780797492509

Edited by
Pathisa Nyathi
Marieke Faber Clarke

Copyright © 2018

Published in 2018
Published by Amagugu Publishers
Typeset & designed by Kudzai Chikomo

All rights reserved. No part of this publication may be reproduced, stored in a retrieval system or transmitted in any form or by any means, electronic, mechanical, photocopying, recording, or otherwise without prior permission of the author or publisher.

CONTENTS

Dedication
page 4

How we came to compile this book
page 6

Inyathi Mission yester-years revisited
page 7

Some useful dates
page 11

Voices from Inyathi School
page 13

Appendix 1: Peter Mackay
page 220

Appendix 2: Outline history of Western-style education at Inyathi Mission
page 230

Books you may like to refer to
page 231

Dedication

This book is written to celebrate the lives of all those who have suffered that Zimbabwe should be free.

"We never fail to tell them" (the Ndebele) "that, though justice is slow in coming, it is coming." Rev. Bowen Rees, LMS missionary at Inyathi 1888 to 1918

"Inyathi School was the only school in Rhodesia that had students who went to prison for political activities". J. Z. Mzilethi

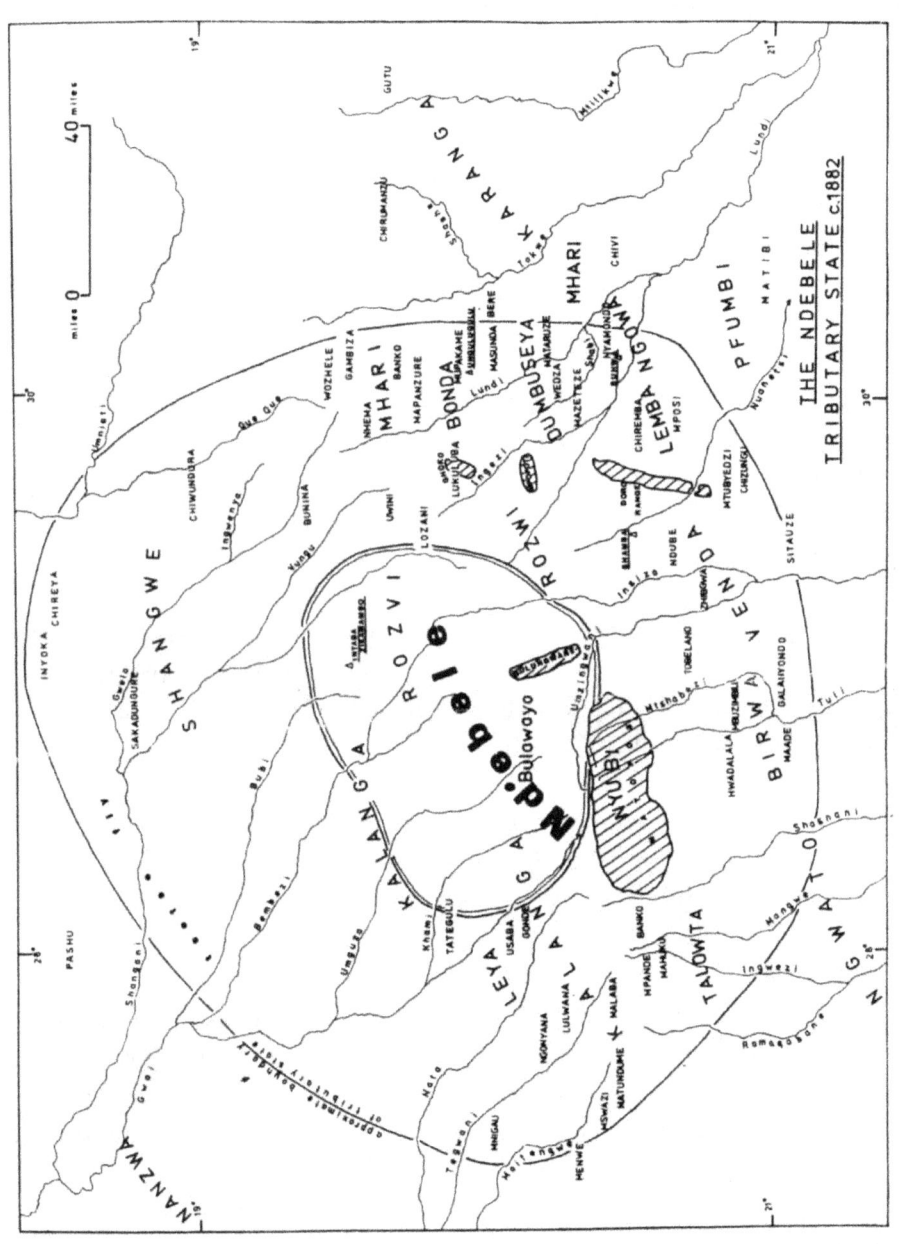

From Cobbing, JRD (1976)

HOW WE CAME TO COMPILE THIS BOOK

When Marieke Clarke taught at Inyathi School starting in September 1963, she was struck by the confidence and assertiveness of her students. She had recently done teaching practice for the Oxford University Diploma in Education in Harlow New Town in Essex. She had been surprised by the sense of powerlessness that pervaded those students. Marieke was born into a British family that was deeply involved in social and political affairs. She soon learned that several of her Inyathi students were actively involved in the struggle for Zimbabwe's freedom and against the white settler regime. She wanted to explore the roots of their confidence. But she had to wait till 2015!

That year Kenneth Maltus Smith, who had been headmaster at Inyathi School when Marieke taught there, died in the UK. His family told her that there were to be two memorial services. One was to be at Inyathi. Two former Inyathi students and Mr Nyathi came with her to that remarkable event. The two former students were J. Z. Mzilethi and Obadiah Moyo.[1]

Marieke asked these three to circulate in the refreshments session after the service itself. The three men, who knew many of the worshippers, chose a range of former Inyathi students who agreed to be interviewed about their experiences at the school. This book is the result.

Originally Marieke had intended only to record the experiences of Inyathi students before 1980. But Pathisa Nyathi and she decided to include material on teachers at the school too.

We wish to thank all the contributors and contacts who have worked so hard on this exciting project. We especially want to thank Joshua S. Mpofu for organising the memorial service and helping put us in touch with his former schoolfellows. We should like also to thank Rodger Muhlwa, Brian Mzana Mthimkhulu and Mrs Musa Dungeni for their help with this project.

---

[1] See the chapters by these friends.

INYATHI MISSION YESTER-YEARS REVISITED
By Pathisa Nyathi

A sombre atmosphere pervaded the colossal dining hall. It was as if there was a coffin that was expected soon to make some appearance before the congregation. The school choir, conducted by a young lady clad in a light blue blouse and grey skirt belted out the tune "I surrender All to Jesus". Three ceiling fans churned the air to mitigate the sweltering heat from the blazing October sun. Now and then bleating goats and croaking hens ruptured the apparent tranquillity beyond the wall of rustic bricks.

The setting is Inyathi Mission of the United Congregational Church of Southern Africa (UCCSA) where last Sunday there was a memorial service for the late Rev. Kenneth Maltus Smith. He was a former head of the school, who passed on in England where he lived in retirement. Inyathi Mission was established in 1859 when King Mzilikazi gave London Missionary Society worker Robert Moffat the use of the land. The mission station that Robert Moffat and his colleagues founded was the first in Matabeleland.

Many former Inyathi School students gathered to remember Kenneth Smith, the man who played no mean part in shaping their future. Among them were the following: Moffat Ndlovu, the former Bulawayo Town Clerk, Rodger Muhlwa, Joshua S. Mpofu, Mrs Gina Madlela, Agrippa Madlela, Mrs Vivien Ncube, Brian Mzana Mthimkhulu, Bekithemba Lusinga, Obadiah Moyo and Zwelibanzi Mzilethi. Also present was Ms. Marieke Clarke from Oxford. She taught at the school from September 1963 to November 1964 when she was deported under the Law and Order Maintenance Act.

Many local people came out to remember the man who played a crucial role in improving the lot of the Inyathi community. Jeremiah Macelegwana Khabo, Josiah Dube, Enoch Bhebhe, Mr Maqeda, Elias Ncube and the local chief Mtshane Khumalo were present. The dining hall was packed to capacity with students who, though they did not know Kenneth Maltus Smith, had learned a lot about the man who was principal from 1957 to 1968. Rev. S. Mhlanga delivered the sermon.

By 11 am the hall was jam packed. Rev. Dr. S. Mpofu, head of the United Theological College and chairperson of the UCCSA Education Board, gave the opening prayer, and later gave an account of what the special Sunday service was all about. What then followed were witness accounts from former students of Inyathi School whom Kenneth Maltus Smith taught.

The first to do so was Rodger Muhlwa who arrived at Inyathi Mission in 1967 to do Form 3. After sitting the Cambridge School Certificate in 1969, Rodger Muhlwa was appointed school clerk. The previous year, Kenneth Smith had appointed Rodger as deputy head boy when Millius Palayiwa Ncube was head boy. The following account is largely drawn from what Rodger Muhlwa said during the memorial service.

From the foundation of Inyathi Mission, lessons were given to local people. Prince Tshakalisa Khumalo's son Dabulamanzi entered the school in 1914. In 1921 a boys' boarding school was opened and by the 1950's it had three distinct components. There was the Central Primary School offering standards 4, 5 and 6; the Industrial School offering post Standard Six training in carpentry; and leatherwork and building. The final component was the secondary school, which opened in 1953 with Peter Sivalo Mahlangu as teacher.

At that time Inyathi School students were doing a three year South African Junior Certificate course. Coming on stream then was the two-year Rhodesia Junior Certificate, to be followed by a further two years leading to the Cambridge Overseas School Certificate.

In 1954, Rev.Kenneth Maltus Smith arrived at Inyathi Mission with his wife Mavis to teach at the secondary school. Mavis Smith taught Mathematics. "Those were the days," recalled Ken Smith in his reminiscences with Rodger last year. At that time school boys used to go and harvest the maize crop on the school farm and to douse the fires on nearby Ndumba Hill.

In 1954 Rev. A. E. Walden, the School principal since 1939, went on furlough (leave) and Rev. John Shaw arrived to become principal. The 1950's were politically volatile. Questions were being posed as to whether African countries were to be granted independence or not. Garfield Todd, the Prime Minister of Southern Rhodesia, gave hope for African advancement through the Five Year Development Plan. There was a lot of hope for African education and political enfranchisement. Soon thereafter came radicalisation of white political opinion.

Prime Minister Edgar Whitehead proscribed the Joshua Nkomo-led Southern Rhodesia African National Congress (SRANC). On 16th February a State of Emergency was declared and on 10 March 1959 one of the Inyathi students, Aleke Banda, was taken by the police and deported to Nyasaland. His parents came from Nyasaland (now Malawi) but he had never been there. Inyathi School at the time attracted students from several countries including Bechuanaland (now Botswana) and Northern Rhodesia (now Zambia).

In 1957 the Inyathi Form 2 boys performed Shakespeare's play *Macbeth*. Walter Mthimkhulu and Noah Maseko were two of the students who took part in the drama, which was performed under the numerous *amachithamuzi* trees in the school grounds. In the same year, the school, with the assistance of the industrial students, started constructing dormitories for girls.

In that year the Form 2 boys sat the Rhodesia School Certificate examinations for the first time. At the end of that year, Standards 4 and 5 were moved to the district schools. Standard 6 was moved at the end of 1961. The principal, Rev. John Shaw was appointed to a post in Salisbury (now Harare) at this time.

When John Shaw moved to Salisbury, Rev. Kenneth Maltus Smith was appointed principal of Inyathi School. At the same time, girls were admitted for the first time.

In 1959 Inyathi Mission celebrated the centenary of its establishment. Sir Robert Tredgold, a grandson of Robert Moffat, presided over the preparations. A commemorative book called "These vessels: the story of Inyathi 1859-1959"[2] by Iris Clinton, was published. This book gave an account of the history of Inyathi Mission. In 1963 a commemorative library was constructed. It contained an original drawing of King Lobhengula, Ndebele spears and shields.

In 1960 Kenneth Maltus Smith went to England briefly and his post was taken, in an acting capacity, by Donald Gray. Meanwhile the London Missionary Society built a new college at Moeding in Bechuanaland. Kenneth Smith was appointed acting principal of Moeding in 1966, the year that Bechuanaland became an independent republic under the leadership of Sir Seretse Khama. In Kenneth Smith's absence, Rev. Harry Undy became acting headmaster at Inyathi. There were a lot of sporting exchanges between Moeding College and Inyathi School: the Moeding netball and soccer teams visited Inyathi.

In 1968 the Principal of Moeding College resigned and Kenneth Smith was appointed in his place, taking up his appointment in 1969. That marked the end of his service at Inyathi Mission.

Several former Inyathi School students went to serve at Moeding College: four of them were Robson Silitshena, Douglas Dube, Enoch Moyo and Siphiwo Bhebhe.

In Kenneth Smith's last years he was actively involved in ongoing efforts to set up the University of Inyathi whose charter is already in place. May his very dear soul rest in peace!

This is a slightly edited version of Pathisa Nyathi's article in the Bulawayo *Sunday News* of 11-17 October 2015. *Editing by Marieke Clarke*

---

[2] This was actually a mistranslation of Chief Mtshana Khumalo's words in 1896. The word *isitsha* referred to Bowen Rees and not to all missionaries.

SOME USEFUL DATES IN THE HISTORY OF MATABELELAND

1787 to 1828: Life of Shaka, King of the Zulus. He ruled 1816-1828.

By about 1840: King Mzilikazi has established a safe home in Matabeleland for the Ndebele people.

1859: King Mzilikazi offers Rev. Robert Moffat of the London Missionary Society the use of the land that became Inyathi Mission.

1868: King Mzilikazi dies in his bed.

1870: His son Lobhengula is consecrated king of the Ndebele.

1880: Queen Lozikeyi Dlodlo becomes queen of King Lobhengula's place of residence, on the site of modern Bulawayo.

1893: Imfazo 1. Cecil Rhodes's soldiers drive King Lobhengula out of his country and begin to make a capital of their own at his old residence.

Two crucial battles: i) Gadade, on November 1st, on the Mbembesi River near Bulawayo.

ii) Pupu (called Shangani by white settlers), on December 5th -12th, in what is now Nkayi District.

1895: Settlers start calling Zimbabwe "Rhodesia".

1896: Queen Lozikeyi as Queen Regent co-ordinates a massive war, Imfazo 2, involving as allies also chi-Shona speaking people. Finally, military forces of the British Empire defeat the Africans.

Early 20th century: Households with large cattle herds start to move away from fertile central Matabeleland.

1909: Queen Lozikeyi requires Rev Bowen Rees of the LMS to give her people help in setting up churches with schools. She wants her people to learn white people's skills and to win back the land that the Ndebele had lost.

1919, 23rd February: Queen Lozikeyi dies in the world-wide Influenza epidemic.

1923: Political power of white Rhodesians greatly enhanced through "self-government" granted by the British government.

1930: The Land Apportionment Act: This sought to separate black people from white people. The law tried to confine Africans to poorer and less land. Meanwhile white people occupied a larger acreage of more fertile land. This Act was a disempowering measure driven by deep-seated racial bigotry, hatred and greed.

1939-45: World War 2. Both white and black Southern Rhodesians fight in the War. So do some white British men, who later get rewarded with land in Rhodesia that had been taken from Africans.

1940's: Largescale forced migration out of central Matabeleland.

1951: The Native Land Husbandry Act: Settlers try to define farming and grazing rights. Africans are provoked but not controlled.

1952: Massive evictions from Filabusi area

1953: Federation of Rhodesia and Nyasaland established by the British against the wishes of Africans in all these territories.

1957: Southern Rhodesian African National Congress revived.

1959: SRANC banned.

1960: National Democratic Party founded

1961: NDP banned.

1961: Zimbabwe African People's Union founded.

1962: ZAPU is banned.

1963: Federation breaks up

1964: August::Nyasaland becomes independent as Malawi

1964: October· Northern Rhodesia becomes independent as Zambia.

1965: White settler Rhodesians declare Unilateral Declaration of Independence from Britain.

1966: First successful guerrilla incursions of the Liberation War. The fighters, who are chi-Shona speaking as well as Ndebele, live in Shangani Reserve for three months and train local people.

1979: Lancaster House Conference.

1980. Zimbabwe becomes independent.

VOICES FROM INYATHI SCHOOL

	Entry date
Prince Dabulamanzi ka Tshakalisa Khumalo	1914
Jeremiah Khabo	1937
Welshman Hadane Mabhena	1938
Peter Sivalo Mahlangu	+-1938
Aleke Banda	1955
Joshua S. Mpofu	1955
Walter Mthimkhulu	1955
Agrippa Madlela	1958
Joshua Mahlathini Mpofu	1958
Moffat Ndlovu	1958
Mildred Mkandla, formerly Ndlovu	1960
Jack P. Nhliziyo	1961
J. Zwelibanzi Mzilethi	1963
Newman Ndlovu	1963
Jaret Sibanda	1963
Musa Dungeni, formerly Mhlophe	1964
Sibongile Maphini, formerly Moyo	1965
Rodger Muhlwa	1967
Brian Mzana Mthimkhulu	1968
Dolly Doreen Ncube, formerly Moyo	1970
Harriet Ncube, formerly Dube	1973
Obadiah Moyo	1973

STAFF MEMBERS
O.N.T.Nhlapo Teacher and principal (Dates not certain)
Marieke Faber Clarke (1963-4) Teacher

PRINCE DABULAMANZI KA TSHAKALISA KHUMALO
Photographed with his father and family. He entered Inyathi School in 1914

The LMS missionary Bowen Rees wrote that year:
"I am thankful to place here on record that I have lived to get King Lobhengula's grandson to come to me at Inyathi for his education. Prince Dabulamanzi is a nice little fellow, nine years of age. He is the son and heir to Prince Tshakalisa.

"In my estimation, this is the biggest victory in one way that the London Missionary Society has ever had in this country and it begins to bear fruit already. Little Dabulamanzi has been here at Inyathi School barely three weeks. The news of his coming has spread like wild fire among the aristocracy of the district. A few days ago, I had two applications for admission into our school from fathers who are holding high positions in the country. This term I have six boarders in school and I find that I cannot very well increase their number until my wife comes out to join me once again in this work....Prince Dabulamanzi is the very image of his grandfather and has pretty little royal ways about him. He does not ride on his high birth. He is as obedient and humble as the poorest child in the school." MFC has edited this slightly.

The prince ran away from Inyathi, but his father sent another son, Prince Qedilizwe, in his place.

The names of these young princes tell people who are prepared to understand that the King Lobhengula was alive. "Dabulamanzi" means "Tear the water apart= cross a body of water". Qedilizwe means "Finish the country" or "Travel a lot". The hidden message is that Prince Tshakalisa, the king's favourite son, crossed the Zambezi River and travelled a long way to visit his father, who took refuge with his royal kinsman Mphezeni in what is now Zambia. See "Lozikeyi Dlodlo, queen of the Ndebele: 'A very dangerous and intriguing woman'" by Marieke Faber Clarke with Pathisa Nyathi, (Amagugu Publishers, Bulawayo 2017 **Third edition**)

JEREMIAH KHABO.
Student, teacher, trade unionist, farmer, politician and businessman at Inyathi
He entered Inyathi School in 1937

Jeremiah Macelegwanja Khabo was born in 1928 and brought up at Inyathi. Both his grandfather and great-grandfather were conscripted into the Mahlokohloko *ibutho*[3]. Jeremiah spent nine years at Inyathi primary school, starting at Grade O. He then did some temporary teaching. He learned some industrial skills at Inyathi School before it became an academic secondary school. He specialised in building. Then he went to Hope Fountain for teacher training. Jeremiah Khabo and Welshman Mabhena were together at Inyathi School, although Welshman, being older, was ahead. Later, Mr Khabo said, "I was teaching at Inyathi with Rebecca Dlodlo when (Welshman and she and Norah and I) were preparing for marriage."

Jeremiah Khabo taught at various schools till 1972. In 1963 he welcomed Marieke Clarke, newly arrived to teach at Inyathi School, into membership of the Southern Rhodesian Teachers' Association. They became good friends and their relationship has lasted (with a break 1964- 1983) to the time of writing. He attended a party she held in her house the night after the Rhodesian police had arrived to remove her. He was one of the first people from Inyathi to stay with her at her home in Crick Road in Oxford. [4]

At Inyathi, Mr Khabo was deeply involved in the District Council. With a few other young men, after UDI in 1965, he queried why the

---

[3] King Lobhengula's *ibutho*

[4] On the day she moved into Crick Road, in May 1968, Rev and Mrs Amos Mzilethi honoured her with a visit, but they were staying elsewhere. Rev Mzilethi was the deeply respected minister of the mission church at Inyathi and had taught Marieke the basics of IsiNdebele. Mrs Mzilethi was a sister of Peter Mahlangu, with whom Welshman Mabhena herded cattle. (See Welshman Mabhena chapter). Robson Silitshena was probably the first Inyathi student to stay at Marieke's Oxford home.

District Commissioner and other white men always headed the council: Mr Khabo and his colleagues won. Previously all the top people on the council except for the chief were white. "Our achievement," said Mr Khabo," was that councillors were elected instead of being appointed by the (white) president."

In 1971/2 Mr Khabo went into parliamentary politics, sitting as a ZAPU supporter who was a Tribally Elected MP. He was a representative for Phakathi constituency. This covered the districts of Shangani, Kwekwe, Lower Gweru, Bubi and Tsholotsho. "Only chiefs and councillors of those districts voted", Mr Khabo said, "but I was identified by the community."

During debates he and his colleagues were looking at atrocities committed under the white regime. These included hanging people underneath helicopters, and showing corpses to schoolchildren. The government would say things such as "See what happens if you support terrorists." In parliament, Mr Khabo said: "When we rule this country we shall not allow such things, "to which Ian Smith made the famous retort that went round the world: "Not in a thousand years."

The parliament was dissolved because of a split in the Rhodesian Front. Mr Khabo was still ZAPU so "I was an unwanted element in that parliament. So the chiefs were assembled at Ntabazinduna and told they would lose their chieftaincy if anyone nominated Khabo. . I had already bought myself a general dealer's store, vehicles and a house in town. That time with a good income enabled me to send all my children to boarding school and to get their training."

After Independence in 1980, Mr Khabo worked for the Organisation of Rural Associations for Progress for more than 17 years. His technical skills made their work outstanding. He retired from ORAP when he was 68. At the same time he was a Board Member of Dabane Water Workshops from its start in 1991 till 2013.

In about 1983, Marieke Clarke and he met up at Oxfam headquarters in Oxford, UK, where she had worked since August 1965. She visited the Africa Desk on impulse. They immediately recognised each other. He had come to tell the organisation about the horrors of Gukurahundi.

"Gukurahundi invaded Inyathi on 25th January 1983," said Mr Khabo. His father died in Bulawayo three days later. "We risked death to bring him home to bury him… At Inyathi Store we were confronted by a roadblock of Gukurahundi troops… I was wearing a complete black suit. The troops spoke threateningly in Shona… In my absence, my brother had been severely beaten. I was harassed at that time for slaughtering a beast for the post-funeral meal… I am a grandson of the Mahlokohloko *ibutho* and I was not going to submit.

"I actually bought the Inyathi store in 1983." By 1989 the store, on the main Bulawayo-Nkayi Road, had become a major social centre where everyone travelling that route wanted to stop.

Mr Khabo was a natural leader of the people of the Inyathi Communal Land.[5] This area had tremendous pressure of humans and cattle. In 1989 it had 6000 people and 1000 cattle in 11 square miles. So there were about 760 people per square kilometre.[6] One of Mr Khabo's greatest achievements was to win the right of these people to run their cattle on what had been the property of the Huckle family: this lay adjacent to the Communal Land. Mr Khabo's achievement was an outstanding example of peaceful community pressure persuading white farmers to part with their land.

"I had known the Huckle family for many years. We African boys had acted as paid ballboys when the parents Huckle played tennis… I started talking to the Huckles shortly after 1980. We had (also)

---

[5] Inyathi Communal Land is the smallest Communal Land in Zimbabwe. In March 2003, Pathisa Nyathi wrote in the Sunday News/Bulawayo Chronicle: "After evictions to Nkayi, for example, some people remained at Inyathi Communal Land hemmed in by white commercial farmers. The remnants came from Emangubeni (Ingubo), Emahlokohlokweni (Mahlokohloko), Embelesini (Imbelesi), Endubeni (Induba), among other places. The chief was Somvubu, son of Mtshana Khumalo."
[6] The highly fertile delta of the Netherlands reportedly had only 407 people per sq km in 2015.

talked with Welshman Mabhena to the Huckles. .. Under government policy, post 1980, local people can no longer be driven away" (if their cattle move on to land that had been acquired by white men.)

"Local people began to cut fences before" (the elderly)" Mrs Huckle died, but once she had died, the fences disappeared immediately. The result is that the cattle of the people of the Communal Land can run anywhere- just what we wanted."

Under Mr Khabo's leadership, a new church, named after King Mzilikazi's royal queen Loziba Thebe okaPhlahana was founded at the Communal Land. This saves its people having to walk a long distance to the mission church.

Compiled by Marieke Clarke after an interview and many conversations.

WELSHMA HADANE MABHENA
Veteran nationalist leader
He entered Inyathi School in about 1938.

Welshman Mabhena's birth date is unknown but he was baptised in 1919 by the LMS missionary Bowen Rees, after whom he was named "Welshman.."

Welshman Mabhena was descended from Ndebele nobility. His grandfather Hadane's brother Sihuluhulu Mabhena was *induna* of the Emhawini *ibutho* at Inyathi and co-commander, with Chief Sivalo Mahlangu, of King Lobhengula's bodyguard. Baby Welshman, son of Makuni Mabhena, was born into a tradition of heroes faithful to their king.

As a boy, Welshman fulfilled his responsibility to herd his family's cattle at Ezinyangeni at Nkayi. He did this together with Peter Sivalo Mahlangu, grandson of Chief Sivalo Mahlangu. (See chapter on Peter Mahlangu). In about 1938, Welshman Mabhena went to Inyathi School where he did Standards 4 to 6. He then became one of the chosen few to go to Tiger Kloof, the prestigious LMS institution near Vrijheid in South Africa. There he studied leatherwork, making modern shoes and bags.

In 1948 Welshman returned to Inyathi to teach these skills. He was also a skilled musician and ran a choir at the mission. Music was very important for the Freedom Movement and was used for building morale. He had been much influenced in South Africa by the African National Congress and would talk about it at Inyathi.

While Welshman was teaching at Inyathi, he met and fell in love with Rebecca Dlodlo, Queen Lozikeyi Dlodlo's niece. Rebecca Dlodlo was a temporary teacher at Hauke when the couple were introduced at a teachers' gathering in Bulawayo. They were married in 1950 by Rev Amos Mzilethi, whose wife was Peter Mahlangu's sister. Welshman and Rebecca had five children.

When Industrial Subjects were phased out at Inyathi, Welshman moved with his family to Highfield in Salisbury (now Harare). He went from school to school, teaching music.

At one time, Welshman worked for a shoe company in Bulawayo. When he had accumulated enough capital, he moved to his rural home at Zinyangeni. He set up his own business and bought a machine on which he made shoes, handbags, belts and suitcases.

Welshman soon became involved in a struggle for African people to claim land at Kenilworth Estates in Bubi District. As a result he had to spend three months in jail.

He helped kindle the fires of nationalism at Nkayi and Silobela. In 1957 the Southern Rhodesian African National Congress was revived under Joshua Nkomo, and demanded independence. Welshman joined the SRANC. When the SRANC was banned in February 1959, and the National Democratic Party was founded in January 1960, Welshman immediately joined. The formation of the NDP marked the beginning of a new era. There was increased African consciousness.

1960 was called "the year of Africa" when many African countries achieved independence. By May 1961, Welshman was the co-ordinator and "super-efficient secretary" of a strong cluster of NDP branches in Nkayi District. As Obadiah Moyo said, "Welshman Mabhena became the torch bearer for resistance and political activism in the whole region of Matabeleland and beyond." (See chapter by Obadiah Moyo). The result was described by the Native Commissioner, Nkayi:
"The efficient administration of the district was attacked from almost every angle, amongst which forms of attack the following might be noted-handing in of dip cards, blockage of dips, refusal to dip, widespread illegal meetings, boycott of cattle sales, mass refusal to

pay personal and arrear native tax, mass refusal to be vaccinated and tuberculosis tested, ploughing at will in allocated areas, and general intimidation throughout the district, making the work of the police in detection and bringing to book extremely difficult." The Ezinyangeni activists had stimulated a populist movement.

The NDP was banned in December 1961 but the Zimbabwe African People's Union emerged soon afterwards. Welshman joined immediately.

Welshman became an outstanding ZAPU leader. The chapters by J. Z Mzilethi and Obadiah Moyo in this book show the great influence that Welshman exerted at Nkayi.

In 1963 Welshman was arrested and accused of moving weapons. Twenty five trucks came to the Mabhena house carrying police and soldiers. Welshman was sent to prison for five years. Altogether he was held in restriction areas and prisons until 1979, with only two weeks of freedom. Mrs Mabhena said that their youngest child "Nozipho was nine months old and at the breast when Welshman went to detention. She had completed Form Four when he returned home." The burden of parenting as well as earning a living fell almost entirely on the mother.

But the harassment and imprisonment of leaders like Welshman Mabhena did not stop the development of the nationalist movement in the Shangani Reserve. Almost every adult in the districts of Nkayi and Lupane was at some time politically active. ZAPU membership reached into every family, if not every home.

Welshman did not regain his freedom until just before Zimbabwe's Independence, but he was busy studying. He attained a Bachelor of Commerce degree and the Fellowship of the Association of Certified Bookkeepers of South Africa.

"I didn't want to find myself left behind others when I came out of prison," he later wrote. "I was sharing a cell with other political prisoners, some from ZAPU and others from ZANU. But I was the only Ndebele there. I learned to be very careful of tribalism."

At Independence, Welshman with other colleagues travelled in ZAPU military cars gathering in ex-freedom fighters. They would convince their colleagues that they had to come to the Assembly Points.

Welshman became a district councillor at Nkayi and was elected chairman. A regional authority for Matabeleland North was soon established and Welshman became chairman of this also. The regional authority aimed to monitor centrally directed development progress.

Prime Minister Robert Mugabe was determined to have a one-party state in Zimbabwe. In January 1981 he demoted Joshua Nkomo, whom he had appointed to the portfolio of Home Affairs. In February 1982, Robert Mugabe sacked Dr Nkomo and most other ZAPU members from his cabinet. This was part of a wider competition over economic resources between ZAPU and ZANU and their guerrilla forces.

Soon the people of Nkayi and Lupane districts were collectively subjected to extreme violence as supporters of ZAPU. A military campaign called Gukurahundi began in January 1983 and then returned before, during and after the 1985 general elections. Political and development activities were completely paralysed. An important aim was to destroy the ZAPU political leadership of the area. Welshman and Rebecca's beautiful home at Zinyangeni was ruined.

Welshman Mabhena was a vocal critic of Gukurahundi. Early in 1983, he was still chair of the Nkayi District Council but failing to organise council meetings. He sought refuge in Bulawayo. Thousands of Nkayi people were leaving their homes to find safety.

Gukurahundi may have cost the lives of 20,000 to 30,000 men, women and children in Western Zimbabwe: it greatly weakened

ZAPU's organisational base and leadership. The repression effectively denied the people of Matabeleland a voice in their own development.

Zimbabwe's second general elections were held in July 1985. ZAPU won every seat in Matabeleland and was returned with an overwhelming majority in both Nkayi and Lupane Districts. Welshman now became MP for Nkayi with 25,874 votes to ZANU(PF)'s 760 and the United African National Congress's 366.

Welshman was an outspoken critic of people who stifled development at Nkayi. A local government officer who worked with him said that "Welshman was keen to see other people develop and yet he was emasculated and incapacitated to do so. Welshman was a member of parliament but he was not in charge of anything. He did not control resources for the implementation of development projects in his constituency."

Welshman's colleague said, "I discovered that Welshman was a great lover of his people. He remained in touch with the people and kept a pulse on his followers. ... He was development-orientated and really wanted to serve his people."

At the 1985 ZAPU Congress, Welshman was elected Secretary-General of ZAPU.

"This meant that he was one of the most powerful people around Joshua Nkomo, and a hard-liner," said a former local government officer. Just after the 1985 elections, "There were dissidents running all over the place" said the then Matabeleland North Provincial Administrator J.Z. Mzilethi (see chapter on him). Mzilethi started his job in September 1985. "But because of the development that we implemented, (the dissidents) did not try to kill me."

"ZANU-PF was keen to poach Welshman to their side," said a district level local government officer. "Always principled and choosing to be with his people, Welshman turned down the frequent advances."

Only a few weeks after the 1985 elections, Welshman with two other ZAPU members of parliament was arrested. It seems that ZANU-PF wanted to punish ZAPU for its success in the elections. After some months in prison far from home, Welshman was released.

Late in 1985, the president of Zimbabwe, Canaan Banana, invited Joshua Nkomo to meet at State House in Harare to discuss the unification of the two parties. Dr Nkomo must have concluded that there was no other way to stop the violence and repression being inflicted through ZANU-PF, except to succumb.

Welshman Mabhena played a crucial role in bringing about the Unity Accord of 1987. He travelled all over the country asking people to join the Unity Process. He said that, when people came together, they could develop the country." The Unity Accord led to the merger of ZANU-PF and PF-ZAPU under the name ZANU-PF and finally brought peace to Matabeleland.

"Welshman thought that things would be sorted out after the Unity Accord," said a retired local government officer. "That's when he joined ZANU-PF, as a way to unify the nation."

Welshman Mabhena served as Governor of Matabeleland North province from 1992 to 2000. His power was limited, since the Five Year Plan had already been made. But the present writer saw with her own eyes in 1989, when she returned to Matabeleland, the great and well-directed development work that was happening under the leadership of the former Inyathi School students Welshman Mabhena and J. Zwelibanzi Mzilethi.

The two men did what they could to promote land reform, the most critical of the province's needs. Welshman wrote to the white farmers of Matabeleland North to ask them to justify how they could each own several huge properties. By 1989, considerable areas of land were slowly being moved from white to African people's control. Jeremiah Khabo (see chapter on him) organised local people at the Inyathi Communal Land and persuaded a neighbouring farmer, Mrs Huckle, to make available her land to Inyathi people for grazing their cattle when she died. This has happened.

J.Z. Mzilethi described Welshman as a "modern traditionalist" who "loved and was interested in everything to do with education." Welshman would talk about the underdevelopment of Matabeleland compared to other regions. He advocated for education and literacy facilities to be made accessible to all Zimbabweans, especially in rural areas, Obadiah Moyo said. (See chapter by Obadiah Moyo). Welshman encouraged Rural District Councils to construct more schools to reduce the distance that children had to walk to school. His intervention saw the number of schools in each district in Matabeleland North Province increasing by at least 30% during the time he was Governor.
"Rural libraries were at the heart of Welshman Mabhena," said Obadiah Moyo.

Welshman was also able to found two important development institutions, namely Hlangabeza at Nkayi and Tsholotsho High School.

"Welshman is best remembered for his fearlessness", wrote Pathisa Nyathi. "He never wavered from speaking out on the marginalisation of Matabeleland."

Welshman Mabhena died in 2010 and was buried in Bulawayo.
Welshman remained all his life faithful to the ideals for which he had sacrificed his precious time. He stood firmly against the perpetration of evil, regardless of who the perpetrator was.

Obadiah Moyo writes: "Welshman Mabhena influenced my mother, me and finally my politically alert fellow students. I hope that more people will see the need to contribute to a better Zimbabwe for ALL- a dream we had as students at Inyathi Mission."

Marieke Faber Clarke

If you want to learn more about Welshman Mabhena, please read our book "Welshman Hadane Mabhena: a voice for Matabeleland". Marieke Faber Clarke and Pathisa Nyathi (Amagugu Publishers, Bulawayo, 2016)

PETER SIVALO MAHLANGU
Entered Inyathi School about 1938

Peter Sivalo Mahlangu, son of Masotsha Mahlangu, was a grandson of Chief Sivalo Mahlangu, co-commander (with Chief Sihuluhulu Mabhena) of King Lobhengula's bodyguard.

The Mahlangus and the Mabhenas say that they came to Matabeleland with Mzilikazi Khumalo, the founder of the Ndebele nation. Mveleleni Mahlangu was in the group, led by Khondwane Ndiweni, who installed Prince Nkulumane as king, thinking that King Mzilikazi had died. When the king arrived, some of the people who had installed the prince fled. Among them was Mveleleni whose wife was pregnant. The child to be born was Mveleleni's last, namely, Isivalo. The name means "Door". Sivalo had no younger sibling because his father had fled back to the Transvaal and never saw his son.

After Conquest, white men occupied the best land in Matabeleland, and elite Ndebele households immediately felt the shortage of pasture, because these families owned many cattle. Chief Sivalo Mahlangu and Chief Sihuluhulu Mabhena were two of the first chiefs to move their cattle and homes from the Ndebele heartland to the "dark forests" of what are now called Nkayi and Lupane Districts. Chief Sivalo moved even before 1910. He moved very reluctantly. His descendant, Chief Solomon Sivalo Mahlangu said, "We still don't like it here" at an Nkayi chiefs' meeting in 1993. The move north had many disadvantages, but it did enable elite families to keep their cattle herds.

In 1909 Queen Regent Lozikeyi Dlodlo required the London Missionary Society worker Rev Bowen Rees to send his most effective colleague, Mathambo Ndlovu, to be her chaplain. Peter

Mahlangu was Mathambo Ndlovu's grandson. Peter's mother was related to Makhaza Nkala, who was killed because he had driven Bowen and Susannah Rees to safety in 1896.

Peter had a sister, Elizabeth, who first married a Mr Ncube and later married Rev Amos Mzilethi, for many years minister at Inyathi and later at Ezinyangeni. When the time came for Peter Mahlangu to herd cattle, he shared the task with young Welshman Mabhena. Peter Mahlangu went to primary school at Inyathi.

The historian and freedom fighter Joshua Mahlathini Mpofu wrote that Peter Mahlangu was a local example of a highly educated person. He came from the north of Nkayi. Peter Mahlangu went to Fort Hare University in South Africa. He gained BA and MA degrees in Education. He was the first man appointed to the secondary school staff at Inyathi when it achieved that status.

Probably Mr Mahlangu was one of the first African Schools Inspectors in the country. When J. M. Mpofu came to know about Mahlangu's achievements, he raised his ambitions beyond those of the teachers whom he had met at primary school. "Many more youngsters wanted to emulate Peter Mahlangu," says J M Mpofu, "but we noted later that he was not politically inclined, unlike Welshman Mabhena."

Peter Sivalo Mahlangu was married to Nursing Sister Poliyanah, (MaMnkandla) who inspired the establishment of Ekuphumuleni Geriatric Home.
Peter Mahlangu wrote two Ndebele books: "Umthwakazi" and "UNcagu kaMbena", both history books.

Marieke Clarke researched this chapter.

ALEKE BANDA (1939-2010)
He entered Inyati School in 1955

By John McCracken, with some editorial additions by Marieke Clarke
John McCracken was Honorary Senior Research Fellow at Stirling University but died on 23rd October 2017 while this book was being prepared.

Aleke Banda was one of the most important and, in many respects, one of the most admirable of Malawi's nationalist politicians. As a young man, aged just 20, he played an important part in the founding and subsequent expansion of the Malawi Congress Party, following the banning of the Nyasaland African Congress and at a time when Dr Banda and most prominent Malawian nationalists were in jail. Later, he became Dr Banda's right-hand man and worked closely with him during the years leading up to Independence and beyond. Like many others, however, Aleke then fell out of favour and was detained without trial for over a decade before making a partial comeback as minister of finance in the first post-Banda government.

Aleke Banda was born in Livingstone, Northern Rhodesia in 1939. He was the son of Tonga parents from the Nkhata Bay district of Malawi who had moved to Northern Rhodesia in search of work. Later, the family moved to Que Que (Kwekwe) in Southern Rhodesia and it was there that Aleke first attended school and had his first taste of politics as secretary of the Kwekwe branch of the Nyasaland African Congress.

From Kwekwe Aleke moved in 1955 to Inyathi School, run by the London Missionary Society near Bulawayo. In an interview with Mzati Nkolokosa in 2008, Aleke stated of his time at Inyathi:

"I was active in school activities and had the opportunity to develop myself in many ways. I was a prefect, secretary of the Debating Society, a Sunday school teacher, editor of the school magazine and secretary-general of the Southern Rhodesia African Students Association which I helped found." 7

In the same interview Aleke singled out the Inyathi headmaster, Rev Kenneth Maltus Smith, as one of the individuals who had most inspired him in life. (Joshua Mahlathini Mpofu relates that, in 1958, Aleke Banda and he formed the Leadership League at Inyathi School and that Aleke was its chairman: "We were training students in leadership."MFC)

Among his other activities at Inyathi, Aleke wrote articles opposing the imposition of the Central African Federation and organised students from Northern Rhodesia and Nyasaland into a secret political association disguised under the title the Bwafano (Unity) Photographic Club. These activities brought him to the attention of the authorities.

On 10th March 1959, Aleke was arrested in the Inyathi School premises and sent to Khami Prison, where he became the youngest detainee (aged 19) alongside many leading Malawian nationalists. After a matter of weeks he was released from Khami and deported to Nyasaland, a country he had never once visited. (Joshua M. Mpofu writes: "The Leadership League ceased to exist when Aleke Banda was arrested.")

Over the next few months, Aleke Banda made his most distinctive contribution to Malawian politics. Based at the Blantyre Mission, where he was given temporary accommodation by the lay-missionary, Albert McAdam and his wife Jenny, Aleke made contact with the Nyasaland Trades Union Congress, one of the few African organisations that had not been banned at this time. From its office, he produced a cyclostyled paper for workers, Ntendere pa Ntichito, which was widened in scope and given a new title, The Malawi News, in December. Meanwhile, he played an active part in

---

[7] Marieke Clarke adds: Joshua Mahlathini Mpofu writes (pers.comm, edited.) "Aleke Banda, who was my senior at Inyathi Secondary School, was Walter Mthimkhulu's classmate there from Form 1 to the time Aleke was arrested in full view of all of us in the school."

persuading the lawyer Orton Chirwa in September 1959 to found the Malawi Congress Party as successor to the banned Nyasaland African Congress. Aleke Banda, aged only 20, became its first secretary-general. When Dr Banda was released from detention on 1 April 1960, Aleke and Orton Chirwa were the first Malawians to meet him. Subsequently, Aleke continued as the editor of The Malawi News, now the official organ of the MCP. It came under the control of Malawi Press Ltd, floated in January 1961 with Dr Banda and Aleke as its only two shareholders.

Over the next decade, Aleke worked closely with Dr Banda, gaining the reputation of being one of his most efficient and loyal supporters. In the run-up to Independence, Aleke accompanied Banda to constitutional talks in London as well as continuing as long-term editor of The Malawi News. Following the death of Dunduzu Chisiza in 1962, Aleke once again became secretary-general of the MCP. He was also appointed by Dr Banda in November 1963 as National Chairman of the newly created Young Pioneers. His greatest regret at this time, so he told Mzati Nkolokosa, was that Dr Banda did not allow him to take up the place at Harvard University, in the USA, that he had been offered in 1961:

"The scholarship was left open for me for four years but each time Dr Banda would not release me. I, therefore, sacrificed my education in the interest of the liberation of our country."

The cabinet crisis of 1964, only a few weeks after Independence, swept Aleke into greater prominence. Up to then, he had been considered too young to hold ministerial office. But now, with virtually all Banda's senior colleagues having resigned or been dismissed, he became a key cabinet minister, serving between 1966 and 1972 as minister for development and planning, minister of economic affairs, minister of finance and minister of trade, industry and tourism.

His very success, however, brought its perils. In 1973 a Zambian newspaper published an article naming Aleke as Dr Banda's likely successor. That year, he was dismissed from cabinet and sent to live in relative comfort in Nkhata Bay. Three years later, Dr Banda relented to the extent of appointing him Managing Director of Press Holdings, by this time the largest company in Malawi. Aleke served in this position for five years, but in the early 1980s fell from favour once again and was sent to the notorious Mikuyu Prison where he was detained without trial for over a decade.

Following his release in 1991, Aleke became involved in the campaign to introduce multiparty democracy in Malawi. He joined the United Democratic Front under Bakili Muluzu and, following the 1994 elections, was appointed minister of finance, a position he held for three years before being transferred to the ministry of agriculture. Meanwhile, Aleke established The Nation as one of Malawi's two leading newspapers. He continued as a minister after the UDF's success in the 1999 elections. However, relations between Aleke and Muluzi became increasingly strained, with the result that in 2003 Aleke left UDF and founded his own small party, the People's Progressive Movement. He died in 2010 after a four-year struggle against cancer. No evaluation of Aleke Banda's political contribution can be made that does not take account of his unfailing loyalty to Dr Banda up to the 1970s and his role in the emergence of an increasingly authoritarian and intolerant strand in Malawian politics. As editor of The Malawi News, he led the way in condemning trade unionists when they attempted to act independently and denounced churches for any criticism they might make of the MCP. As National Chairman of the Young Pioneers, he must bear some responsibility for their increasingly bullying behaviour.

On the reverse side, even Aleke's opponents accepted that he was a man of high intelligence, modest and with a genuine commitment to hard work. Despite his lack of formal higher education, he was widely recognised as one of the most capable ministers to have worked in Malawi. His main political weakness derived from his lack of a popular power base. The UDF, to which he attached himself from 1993, was essentially a southern-based party whose members would never contemplate transferring leadership to a Tonga from the Northern Province. Yet among his fellow-Tonga, he tended to appear as a somewhat distant figure, lacking the deep personal contacts that other leaders possessed.

BIBLIOGRAPHY

There is a useful, although uninspiring description of Aleke Banda's career in Owen J. Kalinga, Historical Dictionary of Malawi, Fourth Edition. This can be supplemented for Aleke's role in the period leading up to Malawi's independence by Andrew C. Ross, Colonialism to Cabinet Crisis and by John McCracken, A History of Malawi. There is also useful material in Colin Baker, Revolt of the Ministers: The Malawi Cabinet Crisis, 1964-1965. For Aleke's own views see Mzati Nkolokosa, 'Aleke Banda: his seven lessons of leadership', online.

JOSHUA S. MPOFU
Entered Inyathi School 1955

I was a student at Inyathi from January 1955 to December 1960. I was not very active politically although in 1958 we formed the Leadership League with Aleke Banda. Aleke was its chairman and I was its secretary. We were training students in leadership, but when Aleke was arrested on 10th March 1959, the League ceased to exist.

At that time I was also chairman of the school's Debating Society, which organised Saturday evening entertainment. I held that post until the end of 1959.

Joshua Mahlathini Mpofu, who was the judge of the Debating Society, became chairman after me. In 1960, I was concentrating on my studies, particularly mathematics. I had decided already, when I was in Form I, that this was the subject I would do at university. In 1961 and 1962, I was at Fletcher High School[8] doing Mathematics, Physics and Chemistry at "A" Level. In 1963 I went back to Inyathi to teach Mathematics. In the first term I was a volunteer teacher. In terms two and three I was employed as a temporary teacher. Mary Austin was my head of department.

The authors are particularly grateful to Joshua Mpofu because he made this book possible. He organised the memorial service for Kenneth Maltus Smith, where the contacts were made with former Inyathi Students.

---

[8] The white minority regime did not want many highly skilled Africans, so Inyathi School management was prevented from having a Sixth Form, though the quality of the students and staff would have justified this.
Brilliant former Inyathi students had to go to sixth forms at Fletcher or Goromonzi schools.

WALTER MTHIMKHULU
Freedom fighter and a leader of the March 11th Group
Entered Inyathi School 1955

I was born at my mother's place, Sinkugwe near Stanmore, Gwanda, on 19th January 1940. My parents were not married. My birth mother was MaNkosi. Her father was a white man who had two children with my grandmother.[9] After I was born, I was whisked away to Lupane to my father's parents and a stepmother: I spent most of my time there. I was like a gipsy. My stepmother MaNdlela was really an angel. My father was working in town: we were living in a detached cottage in Makokoba.

HOW MY ANCESTORS CAME TO MATABELELAND

My great great grandfather Dayise came to Matabeleland on his own. I think he was a healer. He came from Swaziland shortly before Mzilikazi arrived. Dayise immediately joined up with the Ndebele leader.

Dayise had several wives and more than ten sons, including Nqabeni and Wata. My middle name is Nqabeni. Ndawana, one of Nqabeni's sons, was my grandfather. Six of Ndawana's ten children lived to be adults. With his wife MaNdlovu, Ndawana had three sons-Isaiah Joseph (IK), Gerald and Bhola. I was Ndawana's first grandchild and IK's first born.

---

[9] Mzana Mthimkhulu writes: "One incident I recall about Walter's mother (My mother in Ndebele or Mam'omdala/ Senior Mother). She was ill and I visited her at Bulawayo Central Hospital. The Sister asked me her first name.
"I don't know," I said.
"But you said she is your mother".
"You know we never use first names for elders and so I don't know it."
"Describe her."
"An elderly Coloured lady who reads the Bible a lot".
"Aah, that one. We know her! I will take you there."

My maternal uncle refused to receive lobola for my father's family because my mother was Coloured. Before my mother gave birth to me, she had a daughter, my sister Mabel, who is in Canada now. Nqabeni fought in the wars against the whites, but we don't know for how long he was in the army: he had swollen ankles. My grandfather Ndawana died in 1948. When he died, he left a lot of cattle to be shared among his three surviving sons. My stepmother MaNdlela had four children with my father. Two of the sisters are now in Hull.

When I was given my first pair of long trousers, my father said, "Your mother gave them to you." I did not know whether it was MaNkosi or MaNdlela who had given the trousers. So I did not know whom I should thank. I got to know months later when I was visiting Bulawayo. My birth mother asked me if I had received the trousers. I then thanked her. She was based in Gwanda, but working in Bulawayo most of the time.

In Bulawayo, my father earned part of his income from a grocery store at Njube. This had a large catchment area. In effect it was a small supermarket. Our paternal grandmother MaNdlovu told us about our history. She told us about Nqabeni. Our grandfather died too young to be able to do so.

I GO TO SCHOOL AND START MY FIRST REVOLUTION

My first school was an LMS school at Lupane, where I did Sub Standards A and B. The school had no other classes, so I went to stay with my birth mother for further classes. I attended a Brethren in Christ school at Gwanda till Standard 2. In Standard 2, I started my first revolution.

The Brethren in Christ are so dogmatic: they said, "You must be married by the Church". I went to a traditional wedding. It was fun for little boys. There was plenty to eat and lively dancing.

But the Brethren in Christ regarded this as an unholy wedding and had sent spies to see if any of us school students were there. We had just taken our examinations, but we were told that we could not get our results because we had been at the traditional wedding. We were only ten years old, but we were told we had to make 50 bricks as a punishment. I did not have to make the bricks, however, because my birth mother took me to a white senior teacher who did not know about the rule that a traditional wedding was condemned.

I was then sent to Gloag Ranch, a boarding school for Standards 3 to 6. The principal was Rev Samson, who had a son called David: David was the same age as me. He was put in my class. We played together. But David insulted me when I was 11 and I beat him up. He was covered with blood. His father called me in and prayed and said, "I have come all the way from Scotland and you do this!"
I replied, "I did not ask you to come and help me!" Meanwhile Mrs Samson was cooking and we all shared a meal! Rev Samson was a good man but rather superior.

From Standard 6 I went in 1955 to do Form One at Inyathi. Peter Mahlangu was my teacher.[10] I was already politicised: my father, a Presbyterian, had very good English. He had passed Standard 6, possibly by correspondence, and Junior Certificate by UNISA. My father had a car by the time I was at Gloag Ranch.

I START TO BE POLITICISED

I had a totally secure childhood. I was very much loved. The only insecurity was the treatment that we blacks had from the whites. I was angry when a travelling salesman showed contempt for my father.
Because of the domestic security that I enjoyed, I felt that nobody could talk down to me or to my father.
At Inyathi School, from 1955, I started to learn about people, particularly through Aleke Banda.[11] (Aleke and Walter were classmates from Form One till Aleke was arrested. MFC) I wanted to be as organised as he was. He was just slightly older than me. But he was the most organised person I have ever known. He always did what he was supposed to do.

---

[10] See chapter on Peter Mahlangu
[11] See Chapter on Aleke Banda.

Aleke and I had a very good relationship. He once came to Mpopoma to my father's house. Perhaps Aleke was on his way home from Inyathi to Kwekwe at the time.

My father had two cars. I learned to drive when I was about 17 and got a licence at 19. The head teacher of Inyathi School, Kenneth Maltus Smith, used to send me to drive around in a vehicle to do errands for him.

I became aware of class differences between me and other students: I went to Bulawayo for a weekend and the school was closing shortly afterwards. I parked my dad's car at Inyathi, for he knew I should soon be back with the car. What a privilege![12]

At Inyathi School I was playing around and also trying to learn things. I joined many organisations. Probably the first was the Cubs (small Boy Scouts) encouraged by Kenneth Maltus Smith. My first trip outside the country, aged 17, was to a Scout Jamboree at Beira in what was then Portuguese East Africa. My costs were paid by my father. I think that I then began to understand the Portuguese mentality as opposed to that of the British. In Beira, for instance, I could go to places frequented by the whites. But the local people were much worse off than Zimbabweans. The policemen in PEA had bare feet.

MY ACTIVITIES WHILE I WAS AT INYATHI SCHOOL

Maths was my favourite subject. I was very active in a Young Farmers' Club. With Aleke I was active in the Student Christian Movement for three years. Aleke was its Secretary. Miss Joyce Stewart was the senior member. I wanted to be the chairman.

I was getting more and more politicised: "Why were the houses of the white staff at Inyathi better than those of the blacks? " I would ask.

---

[12] In 1963/4 when Marieke Clarke taught at Inyathi School, only one teacher owned a car.. There was perhaps just one car or possibly two cars for the service of the entire mission. It was unthinkable that a student could have the use of a car.

Ken Smith said "We don't make the rules."
Aleke was telling me about his work in the Malawi Congress Party. The day he was taken away, the police deliberately took him from the class. We were stunned. No way could you associate Aleke with violence. We saw that something was wrong. The police must have known his schedules. I met Aleke after he left the school.

REFLECTIONS ABOUT HEADMASTER REV KENNETH MALTUS SMITH AT INYATHI

I liked Ken Smith. He was very informative and very fair. For example, on one occasion we were talking in class about pygmies. I asked if pygmies thought like us. Ken Smith made me realise how prejudiced I was.

We had weekly debates on almost any subject. For a short time I was secretary-general of the Debating Society. I was asked to join the Society after Aleke Banda left.

The school provided a platform for leading thinkers of the time. Joshua Nkomo came with Jason Moyo to Inyathi School in 1958 or thereabouts. Chief Khayisa Ndiweni from Ntabazinduna also visited the school on another occasion.

FORMS FIVE AND SIX AT FLETCHER HIGH SCHOOL

I had applied to Fletcher for A levels and was accepted. I went there in January 1960. About the middle of that year, in June, we had a strike: I was the leader. The school was closed and all the students sent home. I was not allowed to return to the school. The head of Fletcher School was a horrible man, especially compared to Ken Maltus Smith. The Fletcher head especially disliked me because of the strike.

INTO THE WORLD OF WORK

I had to find a job. My father wanted me to work for him, but I said I wanted other experience first. I went to Harare (then Salisbury) to find a job. I worked for the Ministry of Home Affairs as a Pass Officer and was sent to the district office at Gwanda. A man called Trollip was the Native Commissioner. We did not get on well, even though he spoke fluent isiNdebele. The other pass officers were white so I had a separate office. Finally I was sacked and arrived in Bulawayo the weekend of the Zhii Riots.[13]

I went home to Bulawayo to be with my father. I started writing articles for the Daily News. Mijoni was the Bulawayo editor at the time. This was a dream job for me: a full time job as a reporter for the Daily News and the Bantu Mirror.

MY FIRST DISAGREEMENT WITH J.Z. MOYO

There was a riot in Makokoba. I saw Dr Frederick Ashton[14] and interviewed him to ask why people were rioting. Ashton said, "Makokoba is overcrowded". I went to J. Z. Moyo and he said the same thing. My article was printed with the imposed headline: "J. Z. Moyo and Dr Ashton agree". From then on, J. Z. Moyo did not like me.

One of the highlights of my time at the Daily News was meeting South African reporter Keorapatse Kgositsile[15]. He was with the South African anti-apartheid newspaper *New Age*. Keorapatse was on a familiarisation tour of Southern Rhodesia. We were of the same age and had similar political views. I took him round Bulawayo and we had a good time.

In December 1961, the National Democratic Party, of whose Youth Committee I was a member, was banned. ZAPU was rapidly formed. I was asked to work full time for ZAPU's Secretary General in ZAPU's head office in Salisbury. I was Secretary for Information and Acting Secretary-General. I worked closely with Robert Mugabe, a secretive man who never associated with other people.

---

[13] Four days of rioting at the end of July 1960.
[14] Director of African Administration in Bulawayo
[15] Mzana Mthimkhulu adds: The later Professor Kgositsile was an influential South African poet and leading African National Congress member. He died on 3rd January 2018.

ZAPU was banned in late 1962 and the police caught me, like Joseph Msika, at my girlfriend's place near the ZAPU head office. We met to discuss what to do, and decided that some people, like Joseph Msika and myself, should go to Northern Rhodesia on the way to Dar es Salaam. We got arrested at Karoi but were released. We crossed to Northern Rhodesia and Msika went by plane to Dar while I went by the rough road in a UNIP[16] lorry. I had no money for food, but a Rhodesian black man working at Mbeya gave us food and a place to sleep. We got the UNIP lorry the next day.

We reached the ZAPU office in Dar-es Salaam. I was asked to broadcast to the Zimbabwean people inside the country. It was a job. The Tanzanian government paid me. [17]

Towards the end of 1962, Ndabaningi Sithole, who had responsibility for ZAPU outside the country, phoned and said he wanted to send me on a mission into Rhodesia. I was given money to give to Dr Mundawarara, who had a surgery in Luveve. I was told he was doing underground work. Ian Smith was elected prime minister while I was in Southern Rhodesia.

We needed no passport to travel to Southern Rhodesia because the Federation was still in existence. I also had to go to see Joshua Nkomo, who was detained in his home area of Semukwe. I borrowed a car from my father and drove there. I used the pseudonym Cephas Mhlanga.

Sithole gave me a letter for Nkomo, in which he said: "Nkomo, Inkosi kayilwi empini, kuya thina abantu bayo"[18] which was put inside my cigarette packet. I stayed a night with Nkomo. He told me to come back a week later. But there was no car available that day, so I went to Sivako, a Kalanga man, and he lent me a beautiful car. I saw Nkomo, who gave me papers to take back to Dar.

---

[16] United National Independence Party of Zambia, founded 1959
[17] Tanzania became independent in December 1961.
[18] This means: "A king does not go to war, instead it is his subjects who do."

I got as far as Northern Rhodesia and found that Takawira, Sithole (the chair) and Mugabe were advocating the removal of Nkomo, the president of ZAPU. I went over to Tanzania and wondered why they sent me to Nkomo? I was typing up a book for Sithole, but tore it up and gave it to Sithole, who was in the room with Mugabe. I had given money for ZANU to Dr Mundawarara: this was very insulting to me. This was a key part of the formation of ZANU.

I wrote and got paid for articles in the Tanganyika Standard about the formation of ZANU. I called Mugabe a Quisling.[19] I was in Tanzania when ZANU was formed. I became the scribe of J. Z. Moyo, Joseph Msika and Clement Muchachi who were all in Tanzania. James Chikerema and George Nyandoro were locked up just after ZANU's formation was announced. These two pro-Nkomo men then appeared and Nyandoro wrote policy speeches.

There were now two camps in Dar: ZANU and ZAPU. Especially ZANU top men started going back to Southern Rhodesia by *plane.*
ZAPU top people had been talking about sending me to the USA on a scholarship, but I did not want to go. (This was September 1963). I had money in Tanzania coming out of my ears from broadcasting and I was writing articles for the *Tanganyika Standard.* Very reluctantly I went to the USA.

Why was I sent to the USA? Maybe Jason Moyo wanted me out of the way. The Ashton episode was a big issue for him. I detested that Moyo was a very keen Kalanga-ist. I regarded this as tribalism. Nkomo was much more polished and fair, although he was a very keen Kalanga-ist.

FOUR YEARS IN THE USA 1963-7
I majored in Science and Maths. For Communications work, which I did later, the Science and Maths were in fact useful.

---

[19] A traitor who collaborates with an enemy force occupying their country.

My closest friend in the USA was South African student Keorapatse Kgositsile. We had first met in Bulawayo and later in Tanzania when we were both reporters. Now we renewed our friendship in the States. At one time Keorapatse and I shared Hugh Masekela's flat when the latter moved in with Miriam Makeba. Keorapatse and I got very involved with the Black Power Movement. At one time we nearly got killed on the way to a rally in Mississippi.[20]

I finished the four years and told Lusaka: "I am coming back". Back in Zambia I was friends with other ZAPU members: Joshua Mahlathini Mpofu, Rex Nhongo[21], Livingstone Mashengele and Cain Mathema. In fact, Livingstone Mashengele's family and that of my mother lived close to each other near Gwelo (now Gweru).

ZAPU LEADERSHIP:
"SLOPPY MILITARY STRATEGY, ETHNIC REGRESSION AND UNRESPONSIVENESS TO QUESTIONING FROM BELOW."[22]

When I got back from the USA, I wanted to be fit to be a guerrilla, as I had always wanted to fight, and I joined a karate club. I got to Lusaka in December 1967. The ZAPU leadership made no attempt to use people's skills. Exactly a month after I reached Lusaka, I was told, "There's a mission". But I was completely untrained: I had never even handled a gun. I was taken to E Camp on a supply mission to provide ammunition to men at a ZAPU camp near Karoi. In the month before I went to Karoi, Halimana Ndlovu at E Camp showed me how to handle an AK. That was the start of my military training. We left the ammunition at Karoi with no incident.

As I said before, no attempt was made to use people's skills. Colleagues and I who had been in the USA had had four years of Maths and Science. But when we arrived in Lusaka, we were given

---

[20] Mzana Mthimkhulu adds: Keorapatse Kgositsile dedicated one of his poems "My name is Afrika" to Walter Mthimkhulu.
[21] Rex Nhongo (Solomon Mujuru) became ZNA Commander at Independence.
[22] David Moore, Professor of Development Studies, University of Johannesburg

teaching in those subjects by someone who did not even have Junior Certificate.

Another time, just after I returned from the USA, a Zambian[23] army group headed by a white major came to our camp. Most men hid, following orders, but a few of us remained as spokesmen and got arrested and jailed for ten days. (In this group was one woman, Thoko, dressed like a man. The Zambians did not realise she was female. She spent the night with us in the jail.)[24] Chikerema got us released.

While I was in the USA, a big group of activists from Rhodesia (including Dumiso Dabengwa, with Matric, and Akim Ndlovu, who perhaps did not even have secondary education,) was sent to the USSR, mostly in different military fields. Phelekezela Mphoko[25] took the top military position and obstructed anyone else's advance. No one, absolutely no-one else who had been overseas for training was given the opportunity to use that training in the struggle. In the military, a Shona would always be junior to an Ndebele and especially Kalangas were put in charge.

Some colleagues were sent across the Zambezi at Livingstone. It certainly did happen, (as Joshua M. Mpofu writes in his book: MFC), that colleagues crossed the Zambezi and, as soon as they reached the south bank, were caught by the Rhodesians. So the ordinary soldiers started changing the plans they were given, because they did not trust their briefing from Lusaka. The belief developed that there was a spy or spies, possibly a double agent, informing both ZAPU and the Rhodesians.

Another very concerning development was as follows. Military parades were held before a group, led by Philemon Mabuza, from DK Camp, crossed the Zambezi. The Mabuza Group were arguing

---

[23] While Walter was in the USA, Northern Rhodesia became Zambia.
[24] She is now late.
[25] Later Vice-President of Zimbabwe

with Dumiso Dabengwa, asking who made them do the military parades. Dabengwa and Akim Ndlovu ordered photos to be taken. Shortly after the Mabuza Group crossed the river, there were several encounters with the enemy, leading to our men going to Botswana. The biggest surprise was that in Botswana they found the very same photos that had recently been taken at DK Camp. Our colleagues wanted to know: Who else had been shown their pictures? Distrust with ZAPU's leadership grew.

A USEFUL YEAR IN THE SOVIET UNION

Ten of us were sent to the USSR to major in Communications for one full year. We left Zambia in about January 1968 and returned around December 1968. Joshua Mahlathini Mpofu was commander of the group and I was deputy. The Soviets behaved as if I were the commander; Joshua seemed happy that all the problems were lifted from his shoulders onto mine. Rex Nhongo could not understand the course and left before it finished. The Soviets said of Nhongo to Nyandoro when he visited: "What's this chap doing? He's wasting everybody's time." So Nyandoro sent Nhongo back to Lusaka.

When we returned to Lusaka after the year in the USSR, J. Z. Moyo and Chikerema sent our Communications Group to work out of Peter Mackay's private house. (See Appendix on Peter Mackay). After a while we went to a new camp to join up with a group who had been trained in Intelligence. The ZAPU top office appointed me commander. Meanwhile there was in-fighting: you had George Nyandoro and James Chikerema versus Jason Moyo, George Silundika and Edward Ndlovu.

I had been sent to all the ZAPU camps, including the two big ones, DK and East, to set up the Communications. The two big camps were at good crossing points of the Zambezi River. In about 1969, we left someone in each camp to manage Communications. We then went back to Peter Mackay's house in Lusaka, where we were based. It was a very isolated house in the suburbs, so there were no nosy neighbours.

THE BIRTH OF THE MARCH 11ᵀᴴ MOVEMENT, 1971

In 1969, we were reassigned to go to a camp where we were mixed up with the Intelligence experts. Then the idea of the March 11th Movement developed. There was a split between J. Z. Moyo (ZAPU's Treasurer) and James Chikerema, on the one hand, and George Silundika and his group. Chikerema was Vice-President and top of ZAPU after Nkomo: Chikerema was assigned by ZAPU to take responsibility for the military. Chikerema and Moyo excluded George Silundika and other executive members from any knowledge of the military.

Moyo's group was responsible for providing food to certain camps. Chikerema had to supply others. There was a tendency for Moyo to supply Ndebele camps and Chikerema to supply Shona camps. Those of us who came to found the March 11th Movement found this unacceptable.

In the camp that I commanded, the Stompie Camp, which was a small one, I refused to give loyalty to either Moyo or to Chikerema. I said, "We've got Shona and Ndebele men in my camp and we'll take food from either of you."

Those of us who came to belong to the March 11th Movement thought about this issue and I started to write a plan about the situation. I decided we should arrest J.Z. Moyo and Chikerema and their main followers, Dumiso Dabengwa and Akim Ndlovu, (who formed the second rank of Ndebele leaders) and also the second ranking Shonas.

I called a meeting of about 20 people at my camp. They comprised most of the people in the camp including Joshua Mahlathini Mpofu, who was now my deputy: he and I worked very well together.

I started seeing Zambian government people, usually with J. M. Mpofu. We wanted to see if the Zambian government would agree with our plan. The Zambian authorities were in fact very supportive to us: they were upset to see there were two organisations within ZAPU speaking different languages and not talking to each other.

My mission was to try to communicate with all the bigger camps. We dispersed messages to various camps and got very positive feedback. A strong united group led by Philemon Mabuza had spent some months inside Zimbabwe, travelled to Botswana and then returned to Zambia. The Mabuza group joined my group and we moved to F Camp near Lusaka.

Now formally we agreed on action to arrest J.Z. Moyo, Chikerema and all the people in the ZAPU high command: Akim Ndlovu, the commander, Dumiso Dabengwa, in charge of Intelligence, Robson Manyika, Chief of Staff, Phelekezela Mphoko (Logistics). I had recruited Mphoko, when he was working in my father's shop.
The plan was agreed. I resigned my military command so we could correct a political situation. But I was re-instated as commander. I had drawn up a plan to arrest these men.

More people came to F Camp, attracted by what was going on there. I was seeing both J.Z. Moyo and Chikerema, but their group had no counter strategy.

We asked Chikerema, who badly wanted armaments, for transport to fetch heavy weapons from the armouries that Moyo controlled. These weapons were hidden in very difficult country near the Zambezi River.

Former Inyathi student J. Zwelibanzi Mzilethi (see chapter on him) was a weapons expert. He had been trained in arms, explosives etc in the USSR, so we leaders of F Camp involved Mzilethi in collecting these weapons. In our group we had people from Mphoko's Logistics group who had actually stored the weapons. These weapons were hidden unguarded, because apparently the Logistics people thought it was too risky to have the weapons guarded.

So we used Mzilethi's skills and went to the armouries. Mzilethi knew exactly how to check that they were not booby-trapped and we took the weapons. We filled my Land Rover and put some rather useless stuff in Chikerema's lorry. The Land Rover had explosives in it.

We travelled back towards F Camp, but the Land Rover I was driving turned over when the brakes failed going downhill. The lorry was in front of us and stopped in the middle of the road. My Land Rover then ran into the lorry. Very fortunately, nothing exploded. All the weapons were put into the lorry and we transferred ourselves, the weapons and an injured man to the lorry. We poured petrol over the Land Rover so that Mphoko's Logistics people would not find out how their weapons had disappeared.

We took the injured man to Lusaka for medical care. I stayed with him and made up a story about how he had been hurt. As I was admitting him to hospital, Dumiso and J.Z. Moyo turned up for some routine medical problem. They actually carried the injured man into the hospital, not seeing me.

I then went to the ZAPU office and encountered Dumiso and Moyo, who told me: "One of your boys is seriously hurt," and gave me a Land Rover to go and see him in hospital, which I did. I had grown up in Mpopoma with Dumiso and we had always been good friends.

THE MARCH 11ᵀᴴ MOVEMENT IN ACTION

We told the Zambian government that we were angry and frustrated with our leaders, but we did not tell the Zambians what our plans were. We planned in the camps and got our troops –about 40 people- into Lusaka travelling in small groups. Jabulani Mazula was in charge.

Originally we wanted to arrest J. Z. Moyo, Chikerema, Nyandoro, Dumiso Dabengwa and Akim Ndlovu in their offices. But we decided to wait for them in the residential area where all the leaders stayed. (See diagram at end of this chapter, for which Walter Mthimkhulu gave MFC the instructions).

There was only one entrance. Cain Mathema positioned himself near the gate to make things look normal.
Dumiso Dabengwa arrived and stayed outside the gate. He sensed that something was wrong. He tried to run and got badly beaten.

Unfortunately Chikerema and Nyandoro hardly came to Zimbabwe House, and that's why I thought that the attack should happen at the offices. Edward Ndlovu was elsewhere, too, and someone warned him. But my colleagues changed the plans without consulting me. Unfortunately one man escaped. We confiscated the leaders' transport and drove them straight to F Camp.

The following morning, Nyandoro walked into the office and was arrested. He fought hard but was also taken to F Camp. Now we published the arrests. Every Zambian newspaper had my name as the leader of the group.

The Zambian Government had to be involved.

Chikerema went straight to the police, who decided to come to F Camp with him and a frightening number of armed jeeps. Our people spotted them, and sent a message that the police were coming. I ordered the police commissioner to be stopped at the gate and found he was with Chikerema. We were very well armed and even had anti-aircraft guns.

Our commanders, including myself and Joshua M. Mpofu, came out of our camp and walked between the bushes towards the sentries. There we saw the police commissioner with Chikerema. I opened the conversation and said to the police commissioner, "Thank you for bringing Mr Chikerema to us."

The police commissioner then said: "No, he wants to talk, not to be taken in. This is Zambia, you can see we have arms and we will not allow you to take him."

At my signal, the men all appeared from the bushes fully armed, so the police commissioner was tongue-tied. I took Chikerema's hand and took him into the camp and I shoved him in with the other leaders. Our group wanted one or two other people, for instance Stephen Parirenyatwa, the ZAPU representative in Lusaka, brother of the late doctor. Stephen Parirenyatwa was a leading Chikerema supporter. We took them one at a time to bathe in the river, where we all washed. The police commissioner drove away.

I continued to visit the Zambian officials to keep them informed. I met Aaron Milner[26], for example, who was very helpful. We had treated our prisoners quite well.

Finally the Zambian Government decided that Milner would come to our camp to discuss things. He came and we sat down and told him that we wanted to have a conference involving the ZPRA comrades from other camps in Zambia, and that the big group under Ambrose Mutinhiri in Morogoro in Tanzania should be brought in. Milner agreed and talked to the Zambian Cabinet. But they insisted that the Zambians should take all of us to a neutral place and that we must leave our arms at Camp F. We agreed and were taken to a very remote game reserve area at Mboroma.

THE MEETING AT MBOROMA

About 100 of us were at Mboroma waiting with a group of ten to twenty pro- Chikerema and J.Z. Moyo supporters. But no combatants were brought from other camps. Milner flew in. We discussed the conference and he chaired.

The leaders gave their views. Chikerema and J.Z. Moyo walked hand in hand to the podium and said, "We are all brothers. We were chosen by Joshua Nkomo and only Nkomo can remove us." Everybody put their views.

On the final day I had my chance, as the group had agreed in advance. As Philemon Mabuza should have been the chair of the March 11th Committee, he should have spoken, but I was asked to continue.

---

[26] Minister of State in President Kaunda's office. Milner's father was Jewish and his mother an Nguni speaker. (Hugh Macmillan in "The Lusaka years: the ANC in Exile in Zambia".(Jacana Media, South Africa, 2013) p 297

I made 18 points. As we had only the one copy of the paper, and the Zambians took this (see below), we can only recall by memory. But Joshua M. Mpofu has done his best to record what I said.[27] Marieke Clarke has summarised the points for this chapter.

1. Five ZAPU National Executive members in exile[28] accused and counter-accused each other in public in February and March 1970.
2. The Five admitted that there was no strategy to fight the Rhodesia Front regime. All the Five wanted to do was to run a sabotage campaign to frighten the regime into accepting negotiations about majority rule.
   Meanwhile the guerrillas thought they were trained and deployed to launch guerrilla warfare as a first phase to wear down the enemy's military power.
3. The leaders gave no thought to how the fighters and ordinary members of ZAPU would react to this policy.
4. The leaders treated ZAPU like a private company that had gone bankrupt.
5. The leaders made it clear that they were retreating to tribal enclaves.
6. The leaders behaved like antiquated village chiefs and produced no analysis of the military forces in the country.
7. The fallout was the result of the leaders' inability to find a new strategy.
8. So a quarrel developed between them.
9. They used freedom fighters like automatons, not making clear whether the freedom fighters were supposed to be guerrillas or saboteurs.
10. The leaders did not spell out their main goal and fundamental objectives as (for instance) the African National Congress of South Africa had done through the Freedom Charter.

---

[27] Page 174 of J M Mpofu's book.
[28] The 5 were James Chikerema, (Deputy President), George Nyandoro (Secretary General), Jason Z Moyo (Treasurer General), George Silundika (Information Secretary) and Edward Ndlovu (Deputy Secretary General).

11. Fighters considered that the time had come to recognise a guerrilla as a politically motivated fighter.
12. A political programme of national liberation should be based on the premise that liberation was a revolutionary process focussing on the attainment of freedom and social justice in a liberation society.
13. A guerrilla is an angry citizen whose anger is instigated by the injustice of a repressive system of governance in his or her country.
14. A guerrilla is a self-developed politician who volunteers to fight.
15. A guerrilla cannot be treated like a conventional soldier who is expected to follow orders from above.
16. Our leaders failed to understand that our freedom struggle had developed from a civilian-driven struggle for majority rule to a revolutionary process.
17. As the leaders were in disagreement, they could not lead the freedom fighters; the leaders' tribalism disqualified them from leading a revolution.
18. We propose that all five members of the National Executive Committee in exile should be suspended from leadership of the struggle or until a ZAPU elective congress was held.

Milner's demeanour changed that day[29]. I knew something was terribly wrong. I called for a vote. Aaron Milner said, "There's going to be no vote. These are the leaders appointed by Joshua Nkomo and they are going to continue to be your leaders." He seized my paper with the 18 points and kept it.

Milner said: "Who supports Walter Mthimkhulu? Go to the left."
He then said: "Who supports Joshua Nkomo and President Kaunda? Go to the right."

The vast majority came to the "Walter Mthimkhulu" side. Milner then got his security people to arrest us, but there were too many of

---

[29] Hugh Macmillan has commented that Milner was regarded as being pro-ZAPU.Macmillan p 297.

us. A list of "ringleaders" was given to Milner. We were put into trucks and taken to another camp, which we called The Fridge. It was freezing cold at night. The Zambian Government called it the Walter Mthimkhulu Camp. We sent messages to Mboroma to tell the others where we were and that we were safe. The messengers then returned to us at Milima.

Many men- perhaps 40- walked over from Mboroma to the Fridge to be with us. That left about 60 men at Mboroma. A few of the 60 eventually followed Jason Moyo and Chikerema. Some quite influential people were left at Mboroma: they did not all go over to Moyo and Chikerema.

Some men at Mboroma who refused to join Moyo and Chikerema were sent to Livingstone and handed *naked* to the Rhodesians with the message: "These are Rhodesian spies". About 17 men were killed or imprisoned. Some of the group who had been sent to Livingstone were still in prison when I returned in 1978. I fought for their release.

A few others from Mboroma who refused to co-operate with Moyo and Chikerema were sent to prison in Eastern Zambia. Eli Mtetwa fought very well as leader of that group and got the United Nations to bring a court case against the Zambian Government: this was unsuccessful.

We stayed at the Fridge. The Zambian Government took us from the Fridge to prison: a lot of us were taken to Milima Prison, which was an open prison between the Democratic Republic of the Congo and Tanzania. Conditions were quite comfortable: we could play football, for example. Later we were transferred to Livingstone.

While we were in Milima, Peter Mackay came and asked to see me and Cain Mathema. Cain, as one of our Communications men, had often stayed in Peter's house. Peter was very upset at what had happened to us. He said that he was going to London and asked if there was anything he could do.

I briefed him, saying that I thought our chances of getting out soon were very slim: there was no court and we were prisoners at President Kaunda's pleasure.

I said to Peter: "Please do what you can to raise awareness of our situation. The world should know". We arranged a means of communication. Jacob Moyo was Peter Mackay's contact person and got him to be in touch with me, as Mackay and I were already in contact.

Then one man escaped, also called Jacob Moyo. The Zambians moved us to be with convicted prisoners, which made it harder for us to escape. The Zambians took away our shoes. I refused to give up my shoes and two of us were put in solitary confinement. We had no blankets, nothing.

After we had been in solitary confinement for some time, some friendly security guards came at night and brought us blankets and then took them away in the morning. The guards knew us because we had been in the same location for some time. I was in solitary confinement for eleven days: that is a very long time. When we returned to the original place, we still had our shoes. The chance of escape had now passed.

At Milima, there was a big garden which flourished under the expert care of Livingstone Mashengele. We sold food to the wardens. The escapee Jacob Moyo, who was a very big strong man, was brought back after three weeks at liberty. He had become very thin.

We were then brought back to high security conditions at Livingstone. Some of us were beaten up badly, for no reason, by some of the wardens as we arrived. From our cells we could see nothing outside the prison. But Catholic priests came every Sunday to pray with us and talk to us. They took letters for us and received letters for us. We communicated with Peter Mackay, for instance, and the Jacob Moyo who was in Britain.

Nathan Shamuyarira came to see me, but nobody came from ZAPU. Nathan was very helpful: he brought us books so some of our colleagues in jail got their O levels: Cain Mathema was one of them. Gershon Phangwana, an ex Inyathi student, was head of the school. Nathan also went to see the UN Refugee Council in Lusaka. Finally someone from the Refugee Council came to see us and tried to get us support so that the UN could pay our travel costs.

Finally the UK government agreed to take us all: but the Zambian government treated us all as prisoners until we got on to the 'plane. The colleagues who had been imprisoned in Eastern Zambia were released at the same time and taken to the airport.

HUNGER STRIKE AT MILIMA

We had had a failed hunger strike at Milima. We decided to strike till the Zambian Government would decide to do something about the ZAPU leaders.

Some men dropped out of the hunger strike after one day. Everyone eventually gave up except for me. People were circulating around my bed begging me to give up. It really made me cross. I had to go to hospital because I stayed on hunger strike more than a week after everyone else had stopped. There were terrible lice in the hospital, though the prison cells were very clean. A nurse in the hospital was dead drunk and singing. J. Z. Mzilethi talked to a Russian doctor and got himself released because he needed urgent medical attention.

ARRIVAL IN BRITAIN

When I arrived here, I was extremely disillusioned. I felt we had given all we had to reform our Party so that we continued to wage a just war. We had failed. Some of us had even died. Our former comrades now saw us as traitors taking refuge in the land of our former colonisers, We were convinced that *they* were the traitors.

In London we agreed not to be tied by group loyalty. We did not have ZAPU behind us, so we decided that, if it was necessary, we should individually feel free to support other political parties.

Then I joined Abel Muzorewa's United African National Council; Cain Mathema joined ZANU. A few months later I was appointed

UK representative for Bishop Muzorewa. Chikerema and Nyandoro had now joined Muzorewa too. I thought that Muzorewa was a Christian man who was trying to do his bit. I finally met him and he was sound in his own way: he felt there was a way of negotiating with Smith. Muzorewa was also very supportive to the guerrillas in practical ways.

The Geneva conference[30] failed: Smith was very stubborn.

In 1978 I was told to return to Rhodesia. I was scared, but went with some others. I now of course had a British passport. I was Deputy Secretary-General of the United African National Council. Power sharing was agreed. I was elected Deputy Speaker of Parliament and was planning to live in Bulawayo and fly out to Harare at government expense. Muzorewa wanted me to be Minister of Local Government and Housing.

GUKURAHUNDI

By January 1983 UANC was all but dead. I was running the family store in Njube with my brother Mbuso. This was the time when Gukurahundi soldiers were deployed to Matabeleland.

In towns the soldiers did not harm the population. It was a different story in the rural areas. Information on what was going on trickled in through eye witnesses.

AT BUBI...

John Wata Mthimkhulu, a grandson of (my great great grandfather) Dayise, was a trade unionist and political activist all his adult life. He spent ten years in detention with Joshua Nkomo and was one of ZAPU's national executive members. In 1983 John Wata was a councillor at Bubi District. His wife MaSikhosana was a civic leader and a lay preacher of the United Congregational Church of Southern Africa.

On the afternoon of 26 January 1983, Gukurahundi soldiers arrived at the rural home of John Wata and MaSikhosana. The soldiers

---

[30] Late 1976 (MFC)

instructed John Wata to come with them. His wife declared that she would go with him. The soldiers threatened to shoot her, but she insisted on accompanying her husband. The two were made to stand side by side and the soldiers opened fire, killing both in front of their grandchildren.

That evening the soldiers proceeded to Enoch Mthimkhulu's homestead. Enoch was a great grandchild of Dayise and headmaster at Dulutsha Primary School. He was a known supporter of ZAPU, who, during the armed struggle, had supplied guerrillas with food and clothes. The soldiers ordered Enoch's five children to go to another room. The soldiers accused Enoch of supporting dissidents. In front of his wife, MaMnkandla, the soldiers shot him dead.[31]

That night, Mathonsegazi Mthimkhulu, aged 79, buried his son Enoch, his brother John and his sister-in-law MaSikhosana in shallow graves next to their yards. No one came out to assist. People were afraid of attending funerals.

AND AT LUPANE...

Everyone ran from their houses to the bush. My 88-year old Granny MaNdlovu, the widow of Ndawana,[32] was left alone at her home. There was no family member to look after her. I went nonetheless, though I was told that I should be killed. I went to Mzana's father in Bulawayo, and we – the youngest of my aunts and I- went in my car to Lupane. By St Luke's, just by the hospital, we saw the Gukurahundi camp. I stopped the car by the Gukurahundi people, and said, "I am going to pick up a very sick old lady." They said "OK". I took my grandmother. I put her in the back seat of the car and told her to appear very ill.

My grandmother pretended to be dying. The Gukurahundi assumed that I was a doctor and asked where I was taking her to. I said "To Mpilo Hospital". I took my grandmother to Uncle Gerald, Mzana's father, till everything was quiet.

---

[31] Years later, two of the children, Lupho and Mkhululi were students at Inyathi.
[32] The granny who had told Walter as a child about family history. MFC

My cousin's wife MaNkomo, a nurse aid at St Luke's Hospital, was not so lucky. Months after I fetched Granny, armed men knocked at my cousin's house at night. My cousin, an agricultural extension officer, jumped out of the back window and sought help from neighbours, for people who held positions in the community were targets. As my cousin was an extension officer, his life was in danger. When he came back with neighbours, only the children were in the house. MaNkomo and the men were gone. Two months later, a herdboy found the remains of MaNkomo in the bush.

INTO SECOND EXILE

By 1985, Zimbabwe was a living hell for a politician who was not a member of ZANU-PF. I suspected I was under state surveillance. UANC was riddled with state agents and had no realistic chance of ever forming a government. Ben Ndemera, an ex-colleague in UANC, pestered me to follow him into ZANU-PF. During one of our discussions, I said "The spirits of my ancestors will never forgive me if I join ZANU-PF." That was the last time he asked me to join ZANU-PF. In November 1985 I flew out of Zimbabwe to the UK into my second exile.

75th BIRTHDAY PARTY

Birthday celebrations are not a part of our tradition. And so, while I was growing up, I never had a birthday party. As an adult I saw no reason for one. But on 26 January 2015, my relatives and friends threw a surprise birthday party for me. Over 30 of our great-great grandfather Dayise's descendants and about 10 friends gathered at a community centre on Spring Bank in Hull to hug me, dance the night away and wish me a happy 75th birthday. Two cakes, one with an AK 47 outline on top, were baked.

I was touched. For the first time since I was a child, I felt tears gather in my eyes. I had been in prison when my father died in 1972 and so I could not carry out the role of the first son at the funeral. I was in my second exile when both my mothers died. On both occasions, relatives in the UK offered to organise memorial services, but I refused: I just wanted to be alone.

At the end of the birthday party, Terence, my nephew/traditional son threatened that my 80th birthday would be even bigger.

THE MARCH 11TH GROUP LIVES ON

In April 2018 there are about ten, out of the original 43 March 11th Group, still in the UK. Four of us are in England and one is in Scotland. We are lifelong friends. The relationship will never break.
Marieke Faber Clarke interviewed Walter Mthimkhulu in Hull, England, in early April 2018.

Walter Mthimkhulu died in Hull on 7th July 2018. While we mourn his passing, we derive solace and comfort from the fact that his rendition of his role in the Liberation Struggle will reverberate down the corridors of posterity. *Pathisa Nyathi*

Marieke and Pathisa are very deeply grateful to the late Walter and to Mzana Mthimkhulu who has helped greatly with introductions, factual support and editing. Thanks also to Juliet Dube of Leeds and Hull (UK) for her friendship.

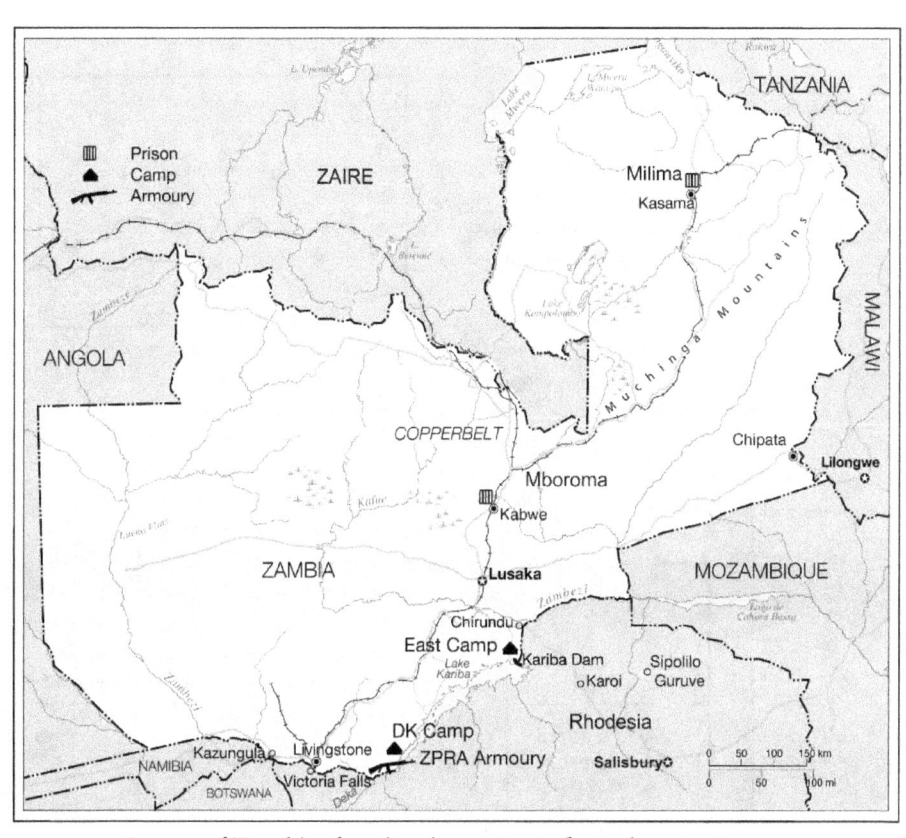

A map of Zambia showing important places in our story

March 11th comrades arrest ZAPU leaders

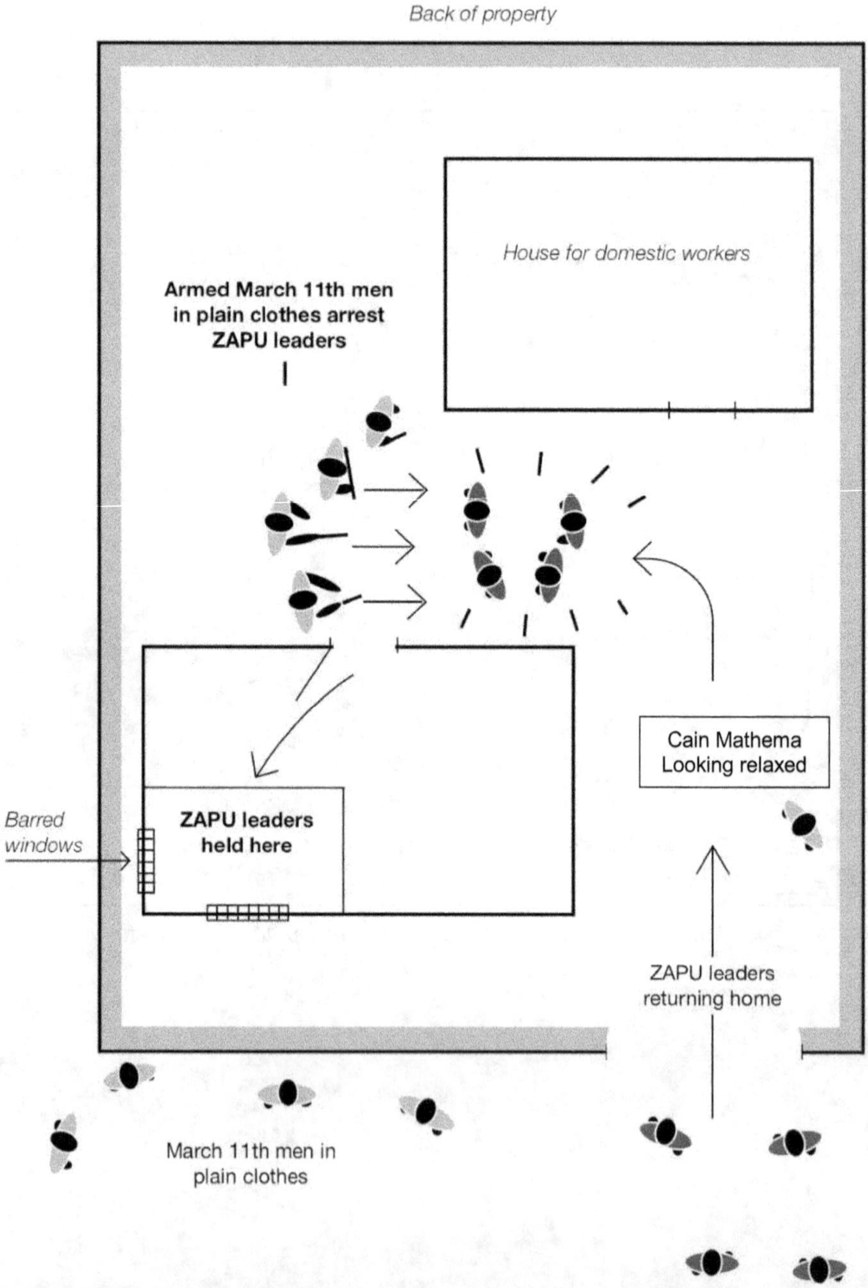

Back of property

House for domestic workers

Armed March 11th men in plain clothes arrest ZAPU leaders

Cain Mathema Looking relaxed

Barred windows

ZAPU leaders held here

ZAPU leaders returning home

March 11th men in plain clothes

AGRIPPA MADLELA
Liberation War Fighter
Leader of the Forum Party
Entered Inyathi School 1958

MY CHILDHOOD AND FAMILY BACKGROUND: CONSTANT MOVES BECAUSE OF EVICTIONS

I was born the third son of a family in Central Matobo in 1937. I grew up there and attended the primary school at Magazana up to Standard 2. In 1945, Central Matobo was declared a "white" area under the Land Apportionment Act of 1930. People started to be removed in 1936 and the removals took place in stages. Most people were removed after the Second World War when British ex-soldiers were coming here. My area was Nkonyana and we were removed in 1952: we were the last group to be removed from Central Matobo. We were told that we were to be removed to Jotsholo at Lupane and from there to Pupu, Gomoza and Kana.

These were tsetse fly- affected areas. The people were crying. I saw my father and my mother crying at the thought. Malaria was bad, but tsetse flies are so big: they were thought to be worse than malaria.
My family was saved from going to these areas by two factors.

We were chiefs of the iHlati *ibutho* who had been reduced to sub-chief status because the man who was occupying that position was an ex-fighter who had fought at Pupu in 1893. He was Mkhotsho Mgadula Madlela, my grandfather. He was an outstanding confident man. Even to the whites, even to the District Commissioner he would show a spear. That's why he was demoted to sub-chief.

We came originally from Enyandeni. We were moved from there to Mgadla (in the Cyrene area) in about 1901-2.Then some people went to Nkonyana in 1918. Then the rest of the community went to Nkonyana. In 1918 we were moved from Mgadla. Part of the

Madlela family went to Nkonyana and part to Magazana in Gwanda. In 1952 those people who had gone to Nkonyana were moved by the police to join the rest of the Madlelas at Magazana. So the rest of the community went to Lupane but not the Madlelas.

I was at primary school at Magazana very near Nkonyana till Standard 2. Then in 1952 we were moved to Gqalaza where I did Standard 3. I lost two years' schooling in 1951-2 because of the moves.

The males in a family went ahead for a year to prepare new places for the household to live. The women would clear the land and holding areas; the small children stayed behind. We were given one year only for this mammoth task. We were moved in lorries, we were three extended families and their belongings. The cattle were moved by train, then moved to another train and then the unfortunate animals had to walk to their final destination. All Madlelas were settled finally in Gwanda, which with Matobo South was the Matabeleland South reserve.

MY FAMILY WAS POLITICAL

I came from a political family. My father, Sheleni Madlela, born around 1898,[33] was very active against the Land Husbandry Act. My father was quite well off, having herds of cattle.

My eldest brother and sister were not as well educated, or as interested in politics, as my second brother Benjamin and I were. Benjamin had been to Tsholotsho Industrial Training School, which, because of water problems, was moved to Mzingwane. My father had also been at Tsholotsho Industrial Training School. Tsholotsho was like Inyathi, another cradle of liberation.

SECONDARY SCHOOL AT INYATHI

I finished my primary schooling at Tegwane in 1957. I liked Tegwane very much but did not get a place at its secondary school: I

---

[33] Mr Sheleni Madlela's name refers to the introduction of the shilling, which happened around the time of his birth.

had lost two years' schooling and was told I was too old (at 16). Tegwane was more civilised than Inyathi at that time. Inyathi was comparatively backward, being called a Bantu Boys' Institute. So I went to Inyathi alone and the outgoing principal, John Shaw, gave me a place. I arrived at Inyathi School with the first co-educational intake, that is, in 1958.[34]

What Inyathi did have was the history of the amaNdebele and the LMS development. I found Inyathi was full of history. King Mzilikazi had given the site to the LMS. My great-great grandfather Mafelilizwe was a close friend of King Mzilikazi. I found this at Inyathi. That made me love Inyathi.

We had an Inyathi School students' league which was very political. It was led by Aleke Banda[35]. The other leaders were Walter Mthimkhulu and Noah Maseko. Aleke's parents were from Malawi and had come to work in the mines in Zimbabwe. He was actually born and bred in Kwekwe. I joined their league. It was voluntary. That's how I was politicised. I read Iris Clinton's book "These vessels" (about the first 100 years of Inyathi mission: see book list at the end of this book) and constitutional history taught by Harry Undy.

J Z Moyo, Lazarus Nkala, George Nyandoro, James Chikerema, one Madzimbamuto and Edward Ndlovu were also in the Inyathi Students' Organisation. Joshua Mahlathini Mpofu joined it too.
In 1958 we students would gather in the hall at Inyathi to hear the Federal News on the radio. When I was in Form One, that same year, I went with Aleke Banda to Stanley Square in Bulawayo. Aleke was bright and politically developed. We went to hear Joshua Nkomo, who had just come back from the World Council of Churches in India. I joined the Southern Rhodesian ANC Youth League at that same time.

---

[34] An extensive building programme was implemented 1953 to 1959.
[35] See chapter about Aleke Banda.

In 1959 the ANC was banned. Aleke Banda was arrested by the Special Branch and had to leave Inyathi School because of his anti-Federation activities. He was taken to Khami prison. The same three people who had interviewed Aleke interviewed Maseko, Walter Mthimkulu and asked Kenneth Smith, principal of Inyathi School, to see me. They interviewed me in Ken's office. Benjamin, my elder brother, a member of the ANC, was arrested and detained. Later he became an executive member of the ANC. He was paying my school fees and the white settlers paid my school fees instead!

In 1961 I had completed Form One. I went from Inyathi to a newly created black polytechnic at Luveve, which is now Luveve High School. This was under two important educationalists: McGuick and Norman.[36]

In 1962 delegates came from Nigeria –one of them was a chief- to speak to us, wondering why we were complaining about conditions, which, they said, were so much better than in Nigeria.

I wanted to pursue academic studies, but meanwhile I became a temporary teacher at Lozikeyi primary school in Njube. I taught up to Standard 5. During that time we went to register at Bulawayo Technical Night School. We were taught by school girls from the high school and some boys went on to A level.
I was recommended to become a clerk at the school, but I transferred to Maphisa School under Stanley Hadebe.

JOINING THE LIBERATION MOVEMENT
In August 1963, I absconded with Japhet Ndubeni Ncube and went to Zambia, Tanzania and eventually to Czechoslovakia where seven of us went to university. We did a Labour Studies course there. I left after one year and returned to Africa, where I spent three months in Cairo, set up the ZAPU office there, then went to Zambia which, since October 1964, was independent.

---

[36] For more about this institution, see Joshua M Mpofu's chapter.

I started work as part of a recruitment effort to find cadres and travelled with them to Tanzania, where they would go for military training. I was also broadcasting news about revolution to Zambia in 1964-5.

In 1966 I went to ZAPU's Logistics Department with Dumiso Dabengwa to deploy people (Atwell Bokwe and Gordon Butshe, for example) to various crossing places into Zambia. We linked up with Peter Mackay[37]. In 1967 I was coming out of an operation in Botswana and was very tired. I found I was offered a scholarship at McGill University in Canada. Meanwhile I was invited to Sussex University in the UK.

I became chief planning manager of the National Railways of Zimbabwe. I became national chairman of the Forum Party.
Interviewed by Marieke Clarke at Bulawayo on 3rd October 2016

---

[37] See appendix in this book on Peter Mackay.

JOSHUA MAHLATHINI MPOFU
"A junior Joshua Nkomo at Inyathi School"

He entered Inyathi School in 1958

Marieke F. Clarke writes:

Joshua M. Mpofu has written a full length work "My life in the Struggle for the Liberation of Zimbabwe". He is the only contributor to this book to have done so. The editors are deeply grateful to him for enabling us to draw extensively on this fine source for the present study. Joshua M. Mpofu has given permission for us to summarise the book.

MY FAMILY BACKGROUND

My family background is of fundamental importance because my father witnessed and got bruised running away from the very first European army that overran his country in 1893, when he was young. My great-great grandfather was Mawondela: my great-great grandmother was Majubane. My great grandfather was Dingimizi and my grandfather was Mjiwa. My father was Mahlathini ka Mjiwa, born 1885 at eMambanjeni (where the current Bulawayo suburb of Bellevue is situated).

Father spent his early boyhood at eMambanjeni till the then royal town of Bulawayo was seized in 1893. Then Grandfather and his family moved to Ematojeni (the Matobo Hills) at a place called Bhedza, now called Whitewater. My father remembered how civilians ran in all directions when Lobhengula's Royal Town was attacked by Rhodes's soldiers. Mostly the civilians ran to the Matobo Hills to hide. Within three years my father witnessed another violent clash of forces when a country-wide African uprising in 1896 took the settlers by surprise. This uprising was crushed by the British army.

My father then grew up in the period when a new European administration was rapidly asserting itself all over the country. Western influence began to cause change to most aspects of African culture. My father went to a mission school when he was about fourteen years old. He finished with a Standard Two and then went to work at the site where the modern city of Bulawayo was being built. In 1921 he married a girl from Entabeni zikaMambo (what English speakers call the Mambo Hills). These are about 16 miles from Inyathi School. My mother's maiden name was Msindose ka Ndubiwa Moyo of the Moyo dynasty and she lived from 1902 to 1970.

My parents had nine children of whom I was the eighth. I was born on 30 September 1939 in the Dimpamiwa village at Nkayi District. Only my younger brother John and I have survived.

MY BOYHOOD AT NKAYI

Nkayi was characterised by vast forest land, with giant trees. The forest land was punctuated by flat savannah grasslands suitable for mixed farming, especially of livestock and small grains. There were beautiful green plains along the river valleys in spring and summer. There was lots of wild fruit in the forest.

At the front of our home, my father had cleared the undergrowth to leave a giant tree canopy forming a natural roof. The cleared spot was an assembly place called "idale" that means "father and sons' assembly place", where every evening my father delivered to his spell-bound sons unforgettable stories of the past.

This is one of those stories: My father talked about African kings and their kingdoms, and would finish by harking back to memories of King Lobhengula's weaknesses in contrast to King Mzilikazi's strengths. My father thought that King Lobhengula should have followed the advice of King Shaka Zulu, who noticed that white men's weapons spat deadly fire from a long distance. My father therefore suggested that Africans should have acquired similar weapons and learned how to use them in order to counter white men's incursions. [38]

---

[38] In fact in 1896 Queen Lozikeyi Dlodlo distributed Martini-Henry rifles and ammunition to the Ndebele troops: this is one reason why the national forces were much more effective in that struggle than in 1893. " Lozikeyi Dlodlo, queen

My father told us that the Europeans would never give up Rhodesia without fighting. "It means that if you boys want to take this country back, you should first acquire some of the white men's good habits and weapons like those that were used to defeat your grandfathers. You will need strong leadership to unite the Africans by bringing various tribes into one nation, as King Mzilikazi assembled several tribes to build the Ndebele nation."

At the age of six, I joined my brother Meshach in herding my father's cattle. My father had nearly 100 cattle. Herding cattle normally started at the beginning of summer, in November, and ended in winter, around the start of June every year. Only after we had fulfilled the responsibility of herding the family's cattle could we go to school. In the 1950's the need to go to school or get a job meant that boys stopped full- time cattle herding when they were about twelve years old.

It was while we were herding cattle that we first saw a "fire-spitting pipe", namely a gun, used by white men to kill animals that were 100 metres away from them. After that eventful day, we herd boys saw these "pipes" many times in the hands of the army and the police. Eventually "the pipes" became a desired tool for Liberation.

Many town people referred to the Shangani Reserve (now Nkayi District and Lupane District) as "Dark forestlands" and the people as "Uncivilised people of the forestlands". Many young people took this as a challenge that they should face head-on by going to school.

YOUNG TEACHERS COME TO SHANGANI

Between 1949 and 1955, many young men and women, aged between 22 and 28 years, came to Shangani to reinforce or replace temporary teachers. There was a boom of qualified teachers who liked smart attire and had immaculate bicycles as well as neat homes. These teachers spoke to each other in English, but without a

---

of the Ndebele: 'A very dangerous and intriguing woman'" by Marieke F. Clarke with Pathisa Nyathi (Amagugu Publishers, 2010, page 154)

trace of self-aggrandisement. They behaved as if they belonged to the local community and gained full respect from the elders as well as the youngsters. One of the teachers' outstanding achievements was to form an association of their colleagues that affiliated to a national body. This made it easy for information to flow through the country systematically.

These teachers won the trust of the communities in which they were located. The young teachers also gained leadership as pioneers of social transformation. They encouraged parents to build new schools and then asked Christian missionaries to provide teachers.

The teachers' comparative economic prosperity motivated parents and children to regard the educators as examples of successful social development and personal integrity. The teachers were also well informed about current affairs. Parents were so impressed at the prospect of the benefits of education that they even sold their cattle to pay school fees to send their children to boarding schools such as Inyathi.

In my youth, African education in the rural areas was provided by Christian missionaries. There were over 50 lower primary schools and 3 higher primary schools. But there was not a single secondary school in what is now Nkayi District.[39] As a result, entry into Inyathi, the nearest secondary school, 80 km away, was extremely competitive. The African secondary schools, which were boarding schools, were open to suitable students from anywhere within the Federation of Rhodesia and Nyasaland. This made the competition even fiercer. But if households could not afford to pay for their children to attend secondary school, the young people would have to leave and try to find paid work.[40]

---

[39] This was because the white rulers wished to limit the number of Africans who were trained to do skilled jobs.(MFC)

[40] Some teachers at Inyathi School contributed towards a fund by which able students from poor homes could receive financial help. (MFC)

If older children were already at school, younger ones sometimes had to wait for their turn to start primary school. I was one of these children. From the age of six, I used to cry to go to school every first day of the first term of the school year. At last, in the middle of January 1950, when I was 10, I was enrolled at Dimpamiwa Primary School to start Sub-Standard A (Grade 1). We soon became literate in English as well as isiNdebele. From Grade 3, students had to speak English during school hours because, from Grade 5, English became the medium of instruction.

In 1953 the hated Federation of Rhodesia and Nyasaland was imposed on what much later became Zimbabwe, Zambia and Malawi.

From 1953 a qualified teacher, my eldest brother Moya Mjiwa Mpofu, was appointed head teacher of Dimpamiwa Lower Primary School. He became my key role model. Moya was the first person I knew to have a "white wedding". This happened on 12th March 1954. One of the outstanding features of the increase in trained teachers and therefore in the number of primary schools was the introduction of "white weddings." These included a Christian ceremony and the bride wore white from head to foot. Every one of my age glued their hopes on that form of wedding. I still remember my father's glowing delight as the bridal procession entered the groom's home in a rhythmic grand march.

DEATH OF MY FATHER

But, only a few months later, my father fell ill and the mission clinic could not save him. He died in August 1954. Following the death of my father, we three youngest brothers feared that our schooling would have to end. But our father's brothers and sister confirmed that Father had told them that the cattle should be used to pay our school fees until we had "finished". My mother had her own cattle so she would benefit from them.

In 1955 we lost my brother Meshach, the one next to me in age. I was devastated, but my mother counselled me to get on with my life.

While I was still at primary school, our geography teacher, Mr Malikongwa, told us to make a change on our map. The country previously called the Gold Coast had become Ghana, an independent African state, in March 1957. This teacher cited some of the leaders of the anti-colonial struggle such as those of Ghana, Kenya and South Africa. Mr Malikongwa also told us about the rebirth of the Southern Rhodesia African National Congress led by Joshua Nkomo and James Chikerema, also in 1957.

ENTRANCE TO INYATHI SECONDARY SCHOOL

In 1958 I was admitted to Inyathi Secondary School where I stayed till I completed my Cambridge Certificate exams in 1961. The school admitted students from all over Southern Rhodesia as well as from the other Southern African countries. As the latter part of the 1950's to the early 1960's witnessed the rapid rise of African nationalism in Central Africa, having students from different parts of Southern Africa gave us the opportunity to share ideas and knowledge.

I do not think that the missionaries deliberately assembled all these different learners to enable them to brew up a conspiracy to overthrow colonialism. But that is exactly what happened at Inyathi School and other secondary schools. The political turbulence that was shaking the shackles of colonialism in the late 1950's to the early 60's reached a climax while I was at Inyathi School.

We deeply appreciated that the missionaries at Inyathi School allowed the evolution of a tradition of free expression of views through debates every Saturday evening. There was one student who was first among equals among the students who discussed and debated. This was Aleke Banda who contributed greatly to students' understanding of African nationalism. (See chapters about Aleke Banda and Walter Mthimkhulu). I was delighted to be at a school where the political issues of the African continent were so hotly debated fearlessly and openly by students. When I was in Form I, Aleke was in Form 3. Though he was just a teenager like the rest of us, his analysis and intellectual portrayal of political issues proved him a motivating firebrand.

When the Federal Government and the three territorial governments banned the three African National Congresses in 1959, they soon all reorganised under new names. The Southern Rhodesian government went further and banned the Southern Rhodesia African Students' Association (SRSA), of which Aleke Banda was Secretary General. At the time, Aleke was in Form 4 and due to take his Cambridge Certificate exams at the end of that year. Everyone expected him to pass with distinction.

But this was not to be: one March morning in 1959, Aleke was picked up from school by two plain clothes Special Branch Detectives. He was sent to Malawi for detention. The arrest left the other students visibly shaken and petrified: our colleague had committed no definable crime except to show his desire for the freedom of African people from the yoke of colonialism.

The Principal, Mr Kenneth Maltus Smith, was asked about the arrest, but he took cover by saying he had no power to question the government on security matters. We were not satisfied by the answer.

After the SRSA ban, its Inyathi branch had to change its name to be called the Inyathi Students' Association (ISA) led by another firebrand, Abel Chanda from Northern Rhodesia.

The arrest of a student at the start of his development as a politician was meant to frighten all youngsters away from political involvement. On the contrary, soon after Aleke Banda's arrest, a few of us noticed widespread anger among the students and that motivated us to be more enthusiastic in support of the Nationalist Movements.

One of my classmates and my friend, Gershon Phangwana, had read about the Chinese struggle against Japanese occupation and the nationalists (Kuomintang) led by Chiang Kai Shek. The Cuban revolution had just occurred. We students at Inyathi were looking for a minimal understanding of clandestine operations under dangerous conditions but without being detected.

My younger brother, John, had just lent me his copy of "The autobiography of Kwame Nkrumah" (1957), but there was not enough material on the underground organisation to rally behind a slogan of "Self-government now". I had some idea about Algeria's war of independence and Nasser's coup in Egypt, but I had no detailed information as to how the campaigns were planned.

A friend in Bulawayo found some reports on what was called "Algerian War" and produced a useful summary for me. We students became very interested in the phrase "underground cells" because it showed how people could operate under cover.

THE INVISIBLE BLACK STONES MOVEMENT

We decided to work only in schools and to cultivate political consciousness among young people, so as to enable them to become part of the national freedom movement. We should do this through connecting to mainstream nationalist organisations in the three territories of the Federation. In 1960 five of us formally established an underground movement called "Invisible Black Stones" with the motto: "The youth of Africa knows no peril".

Gershon Phangwana was appointed to lead the IBS. He was full of constructive ideas on the Liberation Struggle. Other founder members were James Kamanga from Nyasaland (external relations and information),who was a dynamic orator; Douglas Tshabalala who integrated urban with rural students politically, Joshua S. Mpofu who encouraged music clubs in the school to compose and sing freedom songs, and myself, responsible for strategic matters.

Through IBS we clandestinely mobilised other Inyathi students to persuade them to support the African Nationalist movements in each of the three Federal territories. We obtained information from the mainstream political movements in major towns and fed this into our discussions and debates.

The colonial authorities forbade the Freedom Movements to address rallies in the rural areas. So we did our best to fill the gaps by motivating students to convey information about freedom and complement the urban working class in their link with rural peasants in political matters.

When the National Democratic Party was formed, IBS linked up with it through a liaison officer, a Malawian working for *The Chronicle* newspaper in Bulawayo. He sent us a bunch of newspapers every week by post and sometimes he would write a special report for us. He established regular personal contact with the NDP leader Jason Ziyaphapha Moyo. This link with J. Z. Moyo would last up to a comradely level in the armed struggle.

For the 1960 School Year, four members of IBS were elected into the Executive Committee of the Debating Society. I was elected chairperson. In other clubs, such as the Student Christian Movement, two of the IBS members held leading positions. The SCM interacted with students in other schools on a wider scale countrywide, thus becoming a strategic networking web within student organisations in the whole country.

In my final year we recruited and admitted more students into membership of IBS. We chose colleagues whom we found to be on the same wavelength as us concerning political matters. When I stood down as Chairperson of the Debating Society at the end of the second term of 1961, I was succeeded by Moffat Ndlovu, in Form 3, who had just been added to the IBS membership. (See chapter on Moffat Ndlovu).

MODEL PARLIAMENTS AT INYATHI

The school authorities permitted Form 4 students to organise and stage a "Model Parliament". This was based on the political traditions and practice of the British House of Commons. Students were encouraged to act as politicians by forming "political parties" that competed for election as members of "parliament." The election process was managed in a similar manner. The dormitories were delimited into "constituencies" where full-scale campaigning took place behind a "manifesto" and aspiring candidates and their parties canvassed for votes.[41]

A party that won with a clear majority in the "parliament" formed a government and then presented a budget to the elected members of "parliament" on Saturday evening in the presence of all students, witnessed by teaching staff. An imaginary state was usually headed by a titular Head of State with an Executive Prime Minister who would appoint a Cabinet. Presentation of the Budget was followed by a robust debate between the governing party and the opposition party or parties.

On one memorable day, I found myself forming a "political party", which we called the United Peoples Democratic Party. Gershon Phangwana formed another party and James Kamanga formed a third party. It is noteworthy that all three of us were members of the underground IBS, but that on this occasion we were opponents. Debates like these connected us with the real world of political activism, in the Federation in general and what became Zimbabwe in particular. We were able to discern the difference between the practice of democracy in the UK and lack of it in the British colonies.

One of the reasons why it was important to discuss contemporary issues with other students was that they then interacted with their home bases during the holidays. In this way, the students conveyed political messages concerning support for the nationalist movements in championing the cause of African majority rule.

I was responsible for strategy. I had to consider how to stimulate students' enthusiasm to participate in informal discussions. With the support of my colleagues and other students, we created an informal body open to all Inyathi students and called it the Soviet Policy. It had nothing whatever to do with the Soviet Union, but was about social life. The political issues that were covered under the declared

---

[41] As Kenneth Maltus Smith drove Marieke Clarke to Inyathi the first time, he told her happily and proudly about one such "election". "ZAPU" had contested the election with "ZANU", he said, and "ZAPU" had won decisively . MFC

social life issues had nothing to do with Communism at the time. Our Soviet Policy ostensibly focused on matters of morality and romance, as the Policy advocated "One boy one girlfriend" and "One girl one boyfriend". But the underlying purpose was to attract students to assemble informally, so that IBS would have an audience to encourage support for the anti-colonial struggle in all three territories of the Federation. Its "President" was a flamboyant and self-confident Agrippa Madlela, with me as his deputy. (See chapter on Agrippa Madlela).

As most of the discussions were ostensibly about matters of love and romance, attendance and participation were very high and debates were quite robust. The topical political issues could creep in incidentally and would suddenly generate live debates with almost the same enthusiasm as the issues relating to romance.

IBS remained a secret organisation, but the non-IBS students knew a lot about the informal Soviet Policy, which was open to all students. And we made sure that discussion always turned towards the politics of the freedom struggle and the issue of rights and freedoms under colonialism. For instance, students who argued for "monogamous" relationships between boys and girls could argue that this was fair and just behaviour. The principles of fairness and justice could easily be used to bring in political issues: the colonialists preached Christianity (with clear principles of fairness and justice) yet practised injustice towards Africans.

Soon after the formation of the underground IBS and its on-surface auxiliary, the Soviet Policy, the entire School was well politicised and united, regardless of the students' ethnic backgrounds or country of origin. Inyathi Secondary School became an academy of political knowledge and activism in all but name.

Following the Sharpeville Massacre in South Africa (21 March 1960), the Inyathi students paid tribute to the victims.[42] When the three main National Democratic Party leaders were arrested on 19 July 1960, there was a mini-uprising called Zhii ("Down with the enemy") which swept across the City of Bulawayo between 24 and 27 July like a tornado.[43]

Inyathi students passionately supported Zhii, to the surprise of the teachers. In our class, for instance, the English lesson started late because there was an argument with the teacher about the rationale of Zhii. Agrippa Madlela stood up to say that the cause of the uprising was that some people did not see anything wrong with imposing themselves into "someone's home".

The female teacher, a white expatriate, responded that Bulawayo was not someone's home. A jungle of hands was raised as each student wanted to give her their opinion. The student she picked said, "Africa is the home of an African and the intruder is the colonialist; that is why there is violent resistance against the uninvited intruder." The rest of the students applauded their colleague.

By the time I left Inyathi in 1961, I was satisfied that most of the students then at the school would be disciples of the African national liberation movement in their respective countries during the holidays. IBS had grown larger in membership and gender inclusivity.

Gershon Phangwana and I did a lot of political work with students from Lupane District. We formed the Shangani Advancing Students' Association: this galvanised young people and their parents at Nkayi

---

[42] Tom Lodge has written a major book "Sharpeville: an apartheid massacre and its consequences" (Oxford University Press, 2011
[43] For detailed coverage of Zhii, see Terence Ranger's "Bulawayo burning: the social history of a Southern African city 1893-1960" (Weaver Press, Zimbabwe, and James Currey 2010).

and Lupane into activity. The link person in Lupane was Johnson Mkandla, a very passionate champion of African advancement.

I was elected the first Chairperson of the Nkayi chapter of SASA, with Easter Ndiweni as Deputy and Gershon Phangwana as Secretary. We submitted SASA's constitution to the District Commissioners of Nkayi and Lupane: they did not object to it.[44] So, with official recognition, we had leeway to spread the message on political matters with education as a torchlight. We succeeded in wedding education to political consciousness as inseparable twin engines of progress for young people of "Forestland".

From all this, I thought that Kenneth Maltus Smith, the principal, was not fully aware of what was happening in the school. But the testimonial on my school report, with contrasting commendations from the Boarding Master and the Principal, showed that Mr Smith had observed something that he did not like.

The (black) Boarding Master had written something like this: "Joshua was one of the most well behaved boys in the school. His behaviour has been exemplary for other students to emulate."

But the Principal responded: "I hate the Boarding Master's report! Joshua has been exceedingly engaged in extra-mural activities in an unacceptable manner in the school, therefore his behaviour cannot be described as exemplary."

MY POLITICAL ACTIVITIES AFTER I LEFT INYATHI SCHOOL
I arrived in Bulawayo in 1962: ZAPU had been formed on 17th December 1961. African nationalism was at its peak and gaining support from people all over the country.

My family could not afford the fees for Forms 5 and 6, but I spent some time at Luveve Technical College. I was admitted to a five-year

---

[44] SASA invited Marieke Clarke to visit Nkayi, probably in 1964. She consulted senior staff at the school and was told that she would probably be immediately deported if she accepted the invitation, which she therefore declined.

course in painting and decorating. Students did not have to pay tuition or board and lodging fees, because bursaries were available for all LTC students. I looked forward to becoming a qualified artisan.

I was formally introduced to Jason Ziyaphapha Moyo, the ZAPU leader. I became a member of ZAPU in the Youth Wing of Makokoba Branch and attended ZAPU rallies in the townships.

But in the middle of 1962, the Luveve students discovered that the college was not registered as an institution of learning because of the violent opposition of the white unions. There were already two technical colleges for whites (including one in Bulawayo) in Southern Rhodesia, but Luveve was the only such college for blacks. I was one of the black students leading protests against the discriminatory policy. But Luveve Technical College was closed in 1963. The closure of Luveve Technical College showed clearly that Rhodesian whites regarded themselves as the only human beings needing development resources.

In July 1962, aged 22, I was elected to the executive committee of the Makokoba Branch of Bulawayo District ZAPU Youth on the basis of my political record at Inyathi School and Luveve Technical College. With colleagues, I moved from door to door in Makokoba to solicit membership for ZAPU. We were delighted to find that most people in the township had already joined ZAPU and that those that had not yet done so were usually ready to do so.

The most impressive thing we noticed was the unity of people across boundaries of ethnicity and gender. Ethan Dube was chair of the Executive Committee of the Makokoba Youth. Even in early 1962, several activists were being arrested and interrogated under torture. Ethan Dube was one of them, but he had shown amazing bravery. He urged us to resist torture.

In mobilising the masses, one of the issues to share with them was the totally inadequate constitution of 1961, which had been negotiated between the British Government and the Southern

Rhodesian "Government". We explained to the masses that, if ZAPU was banned, perhaps violent conflict could not be avoided.

ZAPU suffered a terrible loss in mid- August 1962 when Dr Samuel Parirenyatwa was killed in a car travelling towards Bulawayo to meet comrades from Nkayi. One of those was to have been Welshman Mabhena. (See chapter on him). The circumstances of the doctor's death were extremely suspicious. The ZAPU lawyer, Leo Baron, told Joshua Nkomo and the white liberal leader Garfield Todd that he had seen Dr Parirenyatwa's body with his hands tied behind his back.

This death was a devastating blow to ZAPU and the nation, because Dr Parirenyatwa was regarded as an intellectual giant.

36 days later, ZAPU was banned. The leaders were banished to their rural homes for three months. We had to do our best to take the organisation underground. When the restriction ended, the leaders decided to go out of the country. In May 1963 there was a major split that further weakened ZAPU and boosted the Rhodesians.

Where should the ZAPU leaders go? Northern Rhodesia, which became independent Zambia on 24th October 1964, was the only possible launching pad from which to unleash a war of liberation on (former) Southern Rhodesia. But would an independent Zambia be strong enough to anchor a project which brought such immense security risks for the newly independent country?

Former Nyasaland gained independence from Britain as Malawi in August 1964 after the hated Federation broke up at the end of 1963. The parties that led the independence struggle in our northern neighbours were allies of the nationalist movement in what became Zimbabwe.

While I had been at Inyathi School, I had learned something about underground cells in the Algerian Liberation War. Now, as an adult, I revisited the Algerian model of creating cells for liberation purposes. I thought that it should be possible to create underground cells from the structures of the banned ZAPU. In my branch of Makokoba, I was the link between the Liaison Officer and several cells of five operatives each. I used the experience I had gained in the Invisible Black Stones (IBS) at Inyathi School. The Liaison Officer for my group was Ethan Dube, a wonderful leader with a commitment to the Liberation Struggle made of steel.

As early as this time, many young people, myself among them, felt that African youths should be sent out for military training in friendly countries. But the leaders said, "Not so fast". Comrade Jo'burg Zwelibanzi Mzilethi, also formerly of Inyathi School, was at the forefront of the movement to present a paper with what was merely a suggestion to our higher echelons. But the official who read the paper while we were waiting looked at us with a stern face and slapped Mzilethi sharply on the cheek. The official destroyed the paper and ordered us never to repeat anything like that ahead of the top leadership. We went away disappointed, but without abandoning our resolve to pursue a military option. (See chapter on J. Z. Mzilethi).

Ethan Dube, our leader, instructed the Bulawayo District Youth Leadership that a minimum use of force against the white government could be undertaken by attacking police stations, police patrols (selectively), infrastructure, bridges, telegraph poles etc. Ethan Dube stressed that people should spend more time on information gathering and verification than on actual operations. Ethan also explained that it was crucial to identify the security and vulnerable features of a target. Though Ethan was just a young civilian, born in 1938, he had a great understanding of these crucial features of military intelligence.

I tried to find a job that would make me appear to be a politically harmless person. I was due to be appointed as a Secretary at a Mission School outside Bulawayo. But a Schools Inspector responsible for recruiting staff suddenly burst out: "I understand that you were making yourself a junior Joshua Nkomo at Inyathi Secondary School. I am sorry we have no place for Joshua Nkomos in our schools." I turned down an offer to explain Rhodesian

Government policy (such as forced land seizures) to rural people, though the job was tempting and paid well.

Finally, in January 1963, I accepted a very suitable job as a clerk in the main stores of Mpilo Hospital in Bulawayo. I was able to buy a car which enabled me to provide transport for our political activities. From there I worked tirelessly to strengthen and fine tune the underground networks in preparation for clandestine activities. One simple way of doing this involved creating social groups, as we had done at Inyathi School, by forming groups *apparently* to discuss romantic matters, but actually to cover our political mission. Now we formed "drinking clubs". These provided a fantastic cover for important things to be "cooked" under that cover, and delivered to the operatives and live cells as feedback between the semi-surface officials and underground operatives. This model, which I had first practised at Inyathi School in the IBS, was repeated in many branches until armed struggle took hold in the countryside with the full support of civilians. These civilians' activities remained unknown to the enemy unless the people concerned were betrayed or caught in the act.

For the sustenance of our activities and operations, we organised fundraising through Mr Ramanbhai Khandubhai Naik and Mr M. K. Naik of Lobengula Street. The two Naiks were businessmen who staunchly supported the Liberation Struggle right from the onset in 1957. [45]

ZAPU SPLIT IN MAY 1963

After the May 1963 split in ZAPU, I was pleased when Joshua Nkomo and colleagues formed the People's Caretaker Council and he became president. The ZAPU structures were revived under a new name. I was elected Chairperson of Makokoba Branch. In August 1963 ex members of ZAPU who had split formed ZANU, which was headed by Rev Ndabaningi Sithole and Robert Mugabe.

---

[45] R K Naik was born in Bulawayo. His first language was Gujarati (a language widely spoken in the west of India to the north of Mumbai). Welshman Mabhena also told Marieke Clarke how indebted ZAPU was to R K Naik. See Marieke Clarke with Pathisa Nyathi: "Welshman Hadane Mabhena: a voice for Matabeleland."

The formation of ZANU led to fierce competition for mass support and a lot of violence. Meanwhile the Rhodesia Front was consolidating its power among the whites, preparing them for a Unilateral Declaration of Independence.

Before the PCC and ZANU were banned in 1964, they sent some of their senior leaders out of the country to set up structures and find sources of weapons to fight the Liberation Struggle. The military wing of the movement was called ZPRA (Zimbabwe People's Revolutionary Army).

In Bulawayo, between 1964 and 1967, colleagues and I established links with a few ZPRA freedom fighters on various missions: Sam Dumaza Mpofu's unit was operating in Tsholotsho, but the Rhodesian forces captured all of them. Lazarus Dlakama entered Bulawayo undetected, until he was caught after several months in the townships. And so on. During this period it seemed that the Rhodesians were in total control of the so-called security situation.

Inside the country, all our youth branches formed special groups organised like regiments with definite command structures. The regimental group was called Zhanda, from the French word for "Policemen," the term used in the Democratic Republic of the Congo during political crises in the early 1960's. We also formed a special group to operate underground: this was called the Formidable Force. These militias were stronger in towns than in the rural areas.

Working with J.Z. Mzilethi, I tried to strengthen resistance in the rural areas. Before the two movements were banned, the Special Branch came to pick me up from my workplace and took me back to my home. They suspected me of possessing guns and explosives. The SB found nothing, but in fact I had, not long before, received hand guns and ammunition. This visit put me on my guard. I continued assisting the infiltration of freedom fighters into the country and received trained personnel from Zambia.

In mid-autumn 1964, I was put under serious interrogation for the first time: since then I have chronic back pain.

UNILATERAL DECLARATION OF INDEPENDENCE, 1965

On 11th November 1965 the Rhodesia Front regime declared Unilateral Declaration of Independence from Britain. Hundreds of us activists were dragged from our workplaces or homes within thirty minutes of the declaration speech. My colleagues and I, served with 30 day detention orders, were held incommunicado in Fife Street police station. We were not allowed to bathe or exercise. We received no visitors. In fact the surface leaders of the PCC and Zhanda were almost totally removed from action on 11th November 1965. When our detention orders expired, some of our colleagues were sent to Gonakudzingwa Restriction Area and some, like me, were released.

MY MARRIAGE TO RATIE SHUMBA (later MPOFU)

After my release from detention, many comrades came to congratulate me. One of these was Munyaradzi Shumba, cousin of a comrade in Mpopoma South Branch. Munyaradzi was accompanied by his sister Ratie, who was waiting for her A level results. It was love at first sight for me and I persuaded my political colleagues to give me time and space to pursue the relationship.

Ratie was dazzlingly beautiful, politically alert and intellectually rich. She became a temporary teacher at Matopo Mission and we soon got engaged. On 16th October 1966 we got married at the Lutheran Evangelical Church at Njube, Bulawayo. I was 27 and Ratie was 21. Getting married to Ratie was the best thing that ever happened to me.

I RETURN TO INVISIBLE ACTIVE OPERATIONS

Soon afterwards I returned to invisible active operations in our cell system. The first significant act I undertook was to print and distribute leaflets: this led to our arrest and a month in solitary confinement. We were released in January 1967. Very soon afterwards, on 23 January, Ratie and I were blessed with a daughter, Nonhlanhla (Lucky Girl). I felt all the more that I must fight for my family and my country. Certain comrades set examples of fearless patriotism, leaving their children and wives to participate in active service for the liberation of Zimbabwe. How could I not emulate them, especially as I was a product of the Invisible Black Stones of Inyathi Secondary School?

Dumiso Dabengwa was an outstanding warrior for liberation and Ethan Dube was a fine mentor and leader.

At the beginning of 1966, the ZAPU leadership started to take armed struggle seriously in terms of adopting long term planning and training large numbers of guerrillas in Algeria, Cuba, Tanzania and Socialist countries. The ZAPU leadership had realised that the Rhodesian so-called security forces could not be shaken by sporadic shooting and explosions.

It had become clear that the British Government would not compel the Rhodesian regime to comply with the principle of "No independence before majority rule". At that time ZAPU was still commanding massive support from the African population, so it was possible to mobilise human resources for military training to raise enough fighters to cause a complete breakdown of law and order in Rhodesia.

Before the "big bang" of 1967, we had received loads of weapons in preparation for armed struggle to be waged by properly trained personnel. The Lusaka ZAPU Office would send someone to Thenjiwe Lesabe or me or any other designated comrade, with a code or password to identify myself when a cargo arrived. I was supposed always to be ready to receive trained freedom fighters coming to me in the evening or night to report their arrival in the city or neighbouring districts.

The delivery of cargo hardly faltered- no lorry driver, so far as I know, was ever intercepted bringing us military equipment- but unfortunately many comrades were captured near the Zambezi Valley before we got a signal of their arrival. It seemed that, further away from the urban hinterlands, especially the areas near Rhodesia's borders, the mass of the people were not politicised enough to understand their role in relation to freedom fighters. The people living in remote rural areas therefore tended to report the arrival of the strangers to the white "Security forces". This enabled the white-led forces to create a "search and destroy" zone by which they surprised the guerrillas and pushed them to a killing ground.

There developed a "saturation" of "buried" military hardware around Bulawayo and Salisbury. For us at the time, it was hard to understand how the weapons reached their destination, but the trained freedom fighters who were supposed to use them hardly passed through the first line of security entanglement near the Zambezi River. Inside Rhodesia many of us suspected that there might be a spy within ZAPU's headquarters in Lusaka.

We became eager to have our Formidable Force trained and incorporated into a regiment ready to fight. But things did not turn out that way. We encountered setbacks from our own blunders because the trained guerrillas who were supposed to use the hardware did not arrive. John Mkandla, Sam Sibanda and J.Z. Mzilethi had to be moved from their homes to hiding places and eventually sent out of the country because two young and inexperienced colleagues were revealing secret information under torture. I myself and other colleagues were arrested in the middle of the night and thoroughly beaten up. None of us, however, gave in to interrogation and we were released.

There was a long-standing plan (dating back to the days of the Federation) that enabled us to "extract" colleagues from danger and send them out of the country. Safety hide-outs were identified in the western and southern routes from Bulawayo to Botswana. Thomas Ngwenya was a driver of a delivery scooter for a pharmacy and a very reliable courier for any consignment, especially distribution of leaflets. He fled to Zambia where he joined ZPRA.

By early 1967 many people began to ask difficult questions such as: "Why are the operations in the struggle slowing down, and so causing the masses to be disenchanted and depressed? "

But just as people were becoming really despondent, we heard that fierce battles were raging in the Wankie (now Hwange) area between the Rhodesian forces and the freedom fighters. Hopes were rekindled, as volumes of information reached the whole country when some of the wounded (black) soldiers were brought to Mpilo Hospital. My comrades selected "safe", totally unsuspected people to talk to the wounded men to find out what had happened. We had no access to white wounded soldiers to hear what they were saying about the quality of fighting and the casualties. But the Wankie battles of 1967 did show that ZAPU had woken up to take armed struggle seriously. African people began to believe that perhaps their forces could win.

The Wankie battles were waged by combined forces of the African National Congress of South Africa- Umkhonto we Sizwe- commanded by Chris Hani- and ZAPU's ZPRA forces under the command of John Dube.

(Marieke Clarke adds: The distinguished historian Hugh Macmillan, in his book "The Lusaka Years: the ANC in exile in Zambia"[46] writes: "The origin of the ANC-ZAPU alliance and of the Wankie and Sipolilo campaigns are obscure... There is little doubt that the pressure for the alliance came from below and resulted from daily contact between rank-and-file members of both {ZAPU and ANC} movements in Tanzania and Zambia."

The detachment at Wankie soon realised that they had been spotted at a point where they had not planned to do battle with the Rhodesian army because they were southward bound.

In 1968, a detachment at Kariba was very severely dislocated by the Rhodesian forces because the detachment suffered a devastating surprise attack soon after crossing the Zambezi River. After that, the survivors split into two groups with one of them surviving until they crossed into Botswana.

(Marieke Clarke adds: The long-serving head of the Rhodesian and Zimbabwean Central Intelligence Organisation, Ken Flower, recalled that the guerrillas were defeated only by the white men's forces' air power,

---

[46] Page 44-45

mobility, and much greater effectiveness in communications and medical services. [47])

In Sipolilo, in 1968, in north eastern Rhodesia, another detachment, made up mostly of ZAPU men and commanded by the former Inyathi School student Moffat Hadebe[48] with Francis Choga established bases for supplies and rear bases for launch and retreat; but they were spotted just before they dispersed for action deep into the country. A massive air raid was launched, resulting in a six hour battle that became known as "the Sipolilo Battle." If Sipolilo had succeeded, ZPRA would have been able to infiltrate deep into the north-east, the eastern and southern regions of Rhodesia. Sipolilo was almost successful, except that the comrades were commanded from Lusaka and not by their commander in the field.

I LEAVE RHODESIA

Exactly one year after my marriage, I had to leave Rhodesia. Since the breakup of the Federation, this had been much more difficult than previously. Travelling to Zambia now required a passport, with a photograph. So comrades who wanted to leave Rhodesia needed to go first to Botswana (independent since September 1966) and then on to Zambia. A previously unknown young woman, MaNcube, saved me from prison or the gallows as we travelled together on the bus. Two detectives came into the bus and looked attentively at every young male passenger. At my urgent request, MaNcube pretended to be my wife and carried on a loud and creative impromptu conversation about private topics. At the end of the journey, she said, "Before I went to Bulawayo, some of your comrades passed through our home and we gave them full support."

---

[47] Hugh Macmillan, "The Lusaka Years: The South African ANC in Exile" page 44.
[48] Moffat Hadebe, who was much influenced by Aleke Banda (See separate chapter on him) had led a group of six men where the first shots were fired in 1964. He escaped from prison when colleagues were recaptured. He went to Algeria for further training and was appointed leader of the Sipolilo Campaign.

I got off the bus at Ntoli in Tsholotsho, was received by my first contact, and then took another bus headed to Plumtree. I was then whisked away by a second contact, who carried me on a bicycle across the Botswana border to Moroka Village, where I had relatives. This escape took place in the second half of October 1967.

My wife received a message that she should come secretly to Moroka Village. She came with our 11 month old baby daughter strapped to her back, crossed the border on a bicycle and spent Christmas with me. She left on New Year's Day and arrived back safely at her destination.

During or about February 1968, at Moroka, there was the deafening sound of helicopters which started hovering over people's homes. My family vowed to protect me, whatever happened. I decided to go to Francistown and ask to be received as a refugee. With considerable difficulty, I was indeed accepted as a refugee. But as soon as the ZAPU office in Lusaka was informed that I was in Francistown, they sent a ticket for me to fly to Zambia, and that happened within a couple of weeks.

WHAT HAPPENED TO MY WIFE AND DAUGHTER?

When I was forced to flee from Rhodesia, Ratie stayed in the country with our daughter. In 1969 Ratie gained a scholarship to train as a physiotherapist at the Royal Orthopaedic Hospital in Birmingham in the UK. Nonhlanhla remained in the care of Ratie's parents in Mberengwa. I later joined Ratie in the UK, so by 1980 (Zimbabwe's Independence) each of us had two university degrees. Then she returned briefly to Zimbabwe. Finally she became Professor and Dean of Community and Health Sciences in the University of the Western Cape. She bore me two more children and died in 2013.

MY ACTIVITIES IN ZAMBIA

After I arrived in Zambia, I was given a thorough de-briefing. I was taken around the large camps to talk to joint fighters of ZPRA and South African ANC's Umkhonto We Sizwe. At the first camp, I was trained to use an AK rifle. I wished that my father had been there to see me holding a pipe that spat fire from a distance. This is what I had been yearning to do since the IBS was formed at Inyathi School.

In no time, I was sent to the USSR to do military training that focused on radio communications (signals). I really felt that ZAPU appreciated the role I played in civilian active service to liberate my country.

With ten other men I was sent to Moscow. I was the leader and Walter Mthimkhulu (See separate chapter) was my deputy. The other men were Solomon Mujuru [49] (Rex Nhongo), Cain Mathema, John Ndlovu, Pius Mashoko, Elias Mugabe, Mgoli Mathuthu, Bhekuzulu Khumalo, Livingstone Mashengele and William Mugwara.

Once the programme, which was useful, was completed, we returned to Zambia to apply our skills. We came back with high morale and ready to get into the war zone. But we had to wait six weeks before our radio equipment arrived. Meanwhile we were at Nkomo Camp outside Lusaka.

It was very unfortunate that, while we were at Nkomo Camp, we experienced extreme brutality from the Lusaka- based Military Administration. For example, one comrade who had sneaked out of the camp to visit a girlfriend was punished by severe flogging and locked up in a dark cell indefinitely, although he was clearly in pain. I was supposed to administer this cruelty, as I was the camp commander at Nkomo. But after my senior commanders, who had given me no chance to raise questions or suggest modifications to the sentence, had returned to Lusaka I ordered the release of the "prisoner:" after all, what he had committed was a minor civil offence. But he had been treated as if he were a traitor.

When the Commander returned after four weeks and found his "should-be prisoner" a free man, he was so angry that he threatened to lock me up. But I stood my ground. Instances of similar brutal treatment of freedom fighters were happening in many other camps.

---

[49] Solomon Mujuru, also known by his War Name of Rex Nhongo, became ZNA Commander at Independence.

Owing to the Military Administration's brutality to comrades, the MA earned the name "Gestapo" after the terrible secret police during the Nazi regime in Germany. Eventually comrades all round expressed disquiet about brutal punishment: it was abandoned during our time.

Once the communication equipment landed at Lusaka, the signals troops were deployed at various fronts. I was sent with two other men from our group of 11 to the eastern front from April to September 1969. Walter Mthimkhulu with three other men from our group remained at the base station at Chelstone, Lusaka.

COMMENTS ON THE DIRECTION OF THE FREEDOM STRUGGLE

To start with, all deployments of large detachments were effectively countered by the Rhodesian forces inside the country. This began to affect the morale of the freedom fighters in the field and in the rear bases. Apparently the ZAPU leaders were unaware that most freedom fighters were deeply agitated by what they considered "grave strategic misdirection" exposed by poor performance in field operations. For instance, the deployment of large military formations in the country, without a clear strategy and tactics to deal with a combined force of heavily armed Rhodesian and South African forces, was a tragic miscalculation by the ZAPU leadership in exile.

Many freedom fighters began to suspect that the ZAPU/ZPRA leadership was merely taking an adventurous gamble.

CRISIS IN THE ZAPU LEADERSHIP IN EXILE
See map of Zambia in Walter Mthimkhulu's chapter.

The first camps to ask the High Command (J.D Chikerema and J. Z. Moyo) to come to explain matters of military strategy were C1 and C2, during or about September 1969. C1 and C2 camps were transit camps on the Zambian side of the Zambezi River. These men held up the Chief of Staff, Robson Manyika, whom they were prepared to keep until the leaders arrived. Chikerema came alone and this compounded the problem.

The first comrade who addressed Chikerema demanded to know what strategy was in place to wage guerrilla war and eventually to overthrow the Smith regime. Chikerema and Manyika could not give satisfactory answers.

J..Z Moyo went alone to DK Camp (opposite the mouth of the Deka River in Wankie/Hwange) to hear grievances. The same questions were asked: the fighters were astounded at the lack of clarity of the High Command and Military Administration on the question of guerrilla warfare, which all of us were trained to carry out in Rhodesia.

The ZAPU leaders surprised the fighters by making further deployments of large detachments without addressing the issues that the fighters had raised in September 1969. At this time Mathema, Mugwara, Mthimkhulu and I were at the main base station at Chelstone, Lusaka, where I assumed command until October 1970.

Both on the eastern and the western front, large detachments were sent on missions that were unclear even to the men directly involved. These units had some of the best fighters in terms of training and commitment to armed struggle. It was a terrible waste of human and technical resources to send well trained and well politicised fighters on an ill-defined mission where there was hardly any preparation with intelligence inside Rhodesia. It was extremely dangerous for large numbers of men to try to cross the Zambezi, which the Rhodesians regarded as their first line of defence. Often the fighters were caught by the Rhodesian forces soon after they crossed the great river.

In 1970, ZAPU freedom fighters were trying to decide what to do about the leaders' disastrous military strategies. At this time, we heard that relations between these leaders had broken down. There was the J. Z. Moyo Group and the Chikerema Group. After furious discussion, four of us were sent to take the leadership of ZAPU in exile and make them explain what they were up to. The messengers were J. Zwelibanzi Mzilethi, Enoch Sebele, Mkandla and myself. We went to Lusaka but only met the J. Z. Moyo faction, because the whereabouts of the Chikerema faction were unknown. So we had to return empty-handed to our furious colleagues.

The freedom fighters felt confirmed in their long-standing suspicion that the leaders were interested in getting to power using the freedom fighters as cannon fodder. The struggle that the leaders were waging was one of sabotage, not guerrilla warfare. And the aim was for them personally to be catapulted into power alongside the colonial masters without changing the state apparatus. The Rhodesian army would remain intact if the ZAPU leaders' plans were fulfilled.

From the days of Aleke Banda at Inyathi School, via the NDP and ZAPU, we were socialised in a culture of regarding one another as sons and daughters of the soil of Africa. But our leaders were now tearing that culture apart as if it were their personal pair of overalls. Something had to be done to avert the impending death of ZAPU and ZPRA if the armed struggle were to be revived.

THE RISE OF THE MARCH 11TH MOVEMENT

It was agreed to create a structure to organise ourselves so as to facilitate communications. We then met at F Camp near Lusaka and elected a leading structure. We called this the Revolutionary Council (RC) and it had 23 members. The 23 elected three men charged with day to day matters of the RC. These three were Zwelibanzi Mzilethi, Philemon Mabuza and myself. Mzilethi was the chairman of the triumvirate and of the RC.

Setting up an RC within ZAPU meant that we were waging a revolution within a revolution, because we had to operate secretly to remove the two factions from the ZAPU and ZPRA leadership. The RC aimed to deliver the five exiled members of the ZAPU National Executive Committee together with the Military Administration to an assembly of freedom fighters at one of the camps. There an all-inclusive ZAPU conference of all ZPRA fighters and civilian branches in Zambia and Zimbabwe would be held. A revolutionary programme and strategy should be adopted to allow us to wage a well- planned guerrilla warfare strategy.

Eli Mthethwa, who had many contacts in the Zambian government, and I were assigned to contact the Zambian government. We should ask their support for a ZAPU conference of all fighters in exile, together with civilian branches and also some comrades to be smuggled out of Rhodesia.

After extensive lobbying, Mthethwa and I told the RC that senior Zambian government officials agreed that we were right. To reinforce our diplomatic offensive, the RC instructed Walter Mthimkhulu and myself to write a letter to the President of Zambia. We did so, submitted the letter to the RC and from then on to the President.

Meanwhile, a nucleus of comrades developed who were convinced Marxist-Leninists. They masterminded the rise of what came to be called the March 11th Movement: at first there was no formal structure.

The freedom fighters decided there should be no military showdown with the Zambian security forces, but the RC said that the fighters should be lightly armed in the operation to take the leaders to Camp F. The task force consisted of Zwelibanzi Mzilethi, (Commander), Walter Mthimkhulu, Job Maphosa and Solomon Ndlovu.

Finally it was decided that the ZAPU leaders should be arrested and taken to the Zambezi Valley. The Organisation of African Unity was the last to be informed about the leadership crisis and the wish of cadres to solve it by a conference of all freedom fighters in external bases.

A secret general assembly of ZPRA fighters was held: agreement was reached that final action should be taken against the five ZAPU leaders (James D. Chikerema, George.B. Nyandoro, Jason Z. Moyo, George Silundika and Edward Ndlovu) in Lusaka. Final action should also be taken against members of the Military Administration.

On 11th March 1971, fighters wearing civilian clothes, but with small arms concealed under their jackets, descended on ZAPU's Zimbabwe House in Lusaka and seized almost all the members of the military administration. Mabuza and I were supposed to surprise and deliver the Chikerema faction in the offices of Oxford Press. George Nyandoro was lured into the ZAPU office and captured but, just as the members of the March 11th group were going to seize Chikerema in Lusaka City Centre, Nyandoro escaped his captors and rushed to warn Chikerema. The J. Z. Moyo faction was already at F Camp. This was only 20 km from Lusaka. Thomas Ngwenya escaped and ran to Professor Makhurane's house, where he alerted Edward Ndlovu.[50]

Chikerema informed the Zambian government about the incident, as did the March 11th combatants. The government had been kept informed about the crisis that had disabled ZAPU for the past 15 months. And the government seemed to understand.

The March 11th combatants continued to try to capture Chikerema and Nyandoro. Finally all five ZAPU NEC leaders were rounded up. On the third day, with these five NEC members and the entire ZAPU military administration under the control of the fighters at F Camp, President Kaunda sent a senior minister, the Secretary-General to the Government, Aaron Milner, to mediate.

The Minister agreed that a conference to be attended by all ZAPU freedom fighters would be held at a venue far away from Lusaka. This was held at Mboroma where Walter Mthimkhulu delivered a keynote speech that he, Gershon Phangwane[51] and I had agreed. Every speaker called for the five NEC leaders to be suspended. (*The details of that speech are in the chapter by Walter Mthimkhulu. MFC*)

---

[50] Pathisa Nyathi, pers comm.
[51] Another former Inyathi School student and a close friend of mine

Walter Mthimkhulu formally moved a motion to suspend the five leaders for the duration of the struggle or until an elective congress of ZAPU was held.

But Aaron Milner intervened and declared that the motion implied that the choice was between rejecting the leadership of Joshua Nkomo and remaining loyal to him. The combatants present clarified that they were still loyal to Joshua Nkomo, but that they rejected the exiled leadership of the five as stated in the motion. Almost the entire force voted for this, to the shock of Aaron Milner as well as the five leaders. But Aaron Milner brushed aside the fighters' pleas for constructive change. He simply said that the Government would ensure that the leaders were reunited, with a fresh resolve so that they could resume the armed struggle.

We were contemplating sending a delegation to President Kaunda to present our case directly: we were concerned that the leaders, who were divided, were being treated with kid gloves and no progress was being made.

But soon the Zambian Paramilitary Police assembled us and announced that the trained cadres should be separated from the recruits. Eventually Zambian forces took us away to be detained at an undisclosed location. Tensions rose very high, but we still persuaded the comrades not to use force against the Zambian authorities. Finally 41 of us were taken away to Kasama, a town near the Tanzanian frontier. Two of the comrades had escaped before we got so far.

This detention of the core leadership of the combat fighters marked the end of the road for ZAPU as a leading engine of national liberation. Some of us thought that when the Zambians detained us they placed a barrier against our resumption of active service in the liberation of our country. 39 of us were taken to Milima Prison while the rest of the fighters stayed at Mboroma.

The Zambian government tried to order the rest of the comrades back to the leaders and even attempted to use force, but without success. Some men escaped from Mboroma and mingled with the Zambian population while others joined ZANU.

129 men who remained at Mboroma were driven to the Rhodesian border and handed over to the Smith regime. How could Zambia's leaders do this? ZPRA's freedom fighters were drilled to respect the Zambian authorities and had adhered to this tradition.

The divided ZAPU leaders then split into factions: one formed a Front for the Liberation of Zimbabwe (FROLIZI) and the other remained in the dormant ZAPU mainstream until they teamed up with ZANU to form Joint Military Command.

What a great opportunity the Zambian Government missed! Four years later ZANLA and ZPRA combined to form the Zimbabwe People's Army to resume the struggle without political leaders. ZIPA was lucky because they were close to President Samora Machel of Mozambique: President Kaunda could have played the same role.

MILIMA PRISON

We 34 combatants were welcomed by the superintendent of the prison rather as if he were the principal of a teacher training college. The 34 men were divided into two groups and met to discuss how we could get out of prison. It was then we formally adopted the name of the March 11th Movement. A new leadership was elected. This five man Executive Committee consisted of Philemon Mabuza (Chair), with Matshikidze Gutu as his deputy, myself as secretary, Zwelibanzi Mzilethi and Jabulani Mazula. Livingstone Mashengele, who had qualifications in agriculture, managed the garden most efficiently.

We decided to write a letter to the President of Zambia explaining that we wanted to resume the armed struggle. The prison warders at Milima were quite aware of the struggle in Zimbabwe and genuinely sympathetic to us. They helped us as much as possible.

In Milima Prison, the comrades who had come under the influence of Marxist-Leninism met again. We decided that our national revolution would be based on the ideology of Socialism and encouraged comrades to study Marxist-Leninist literature. In the prison, a structured core organisation was formed. It would politicise comrades behind the scenes and then admit those of them whom we regarded as qualified to be part of the core, more or less like the IBS within the student association at Inyathi Secondary School in the early 1960's.

I was elected the first chairman of the core circle and Matsikidze Gutu was my deputy. The Core circle's first task was to endeavour to engulf the entire March 11th movement into a progressive Marxist movement. Unfortunately, about a year after we entered Milima Prison, the March 11th movement split.
Though we had visitors from the two ZAPU leaders' delegations, we decided not to join them.

STUDIES IN PRISON

One of the most important decisions we took was to start a school with teaching from the lowest grade to A level. All comrades with O level and above were assigned to teach the rest of the comrades. Nathan Shamuyarira's FROLIZI sent us a wide range of books, for which we were very grateful, though we regarded his organisation's outlook as tribal and shallow in terms of national goals. Finally, many comrades gained qualifications in prison.

DISTURBING DEVELOPMENTS

A few months after we were taken to Milima Prison, one of our comrades escaped without notifying us. We were made to suffer because the prison authorities believed that the escape was collectively planned. During the comrades' exchanges with the officers, the latter came to realise that we were desperate.

At this point we heard that 129 (3 detachments) of our comrades who had been with us at Mboroma had been deported to Rhodesia. We then realised that the government of Zambia had failed to unify our leaders without our being involved.

However, the escaped comrade was recaptured and the situation eventually returned to normal; the comrades came together as one group. We then devised a plan that one man should escape legally. He should fight for our release by involving humanitarian organisations and other countries to put pressure on the Zambian government to release us, so we could return to the armed struggle.

We went on a prolonged hunger strike that took three full weeks. At the end of the third week, some of us became ill and were sent to Kasama Hospital. We assigned Zwelibanzi Mzilethi to cultivate a close friendship with the doctor, and persuade her to create the conditions that would persuade the Zambian government to release him soonest. She reluctantly agreed, as she feared that he would die. She also recommended that Mzilethi's condition could only be treated overseas. The Zambian government accepted the doctor's recommendations and issued him with a passport to travel to the UK.

On arrival in the UK, Mzilethi linked up with my wife Ratie, who was a student at Birmingham Orthopaedic Hospital. The two of them worked together very effectively.

SUDDEN TRANSFER TO A PRISON NEAR THE RHODESIAN BORDER

Meanwhile our hopes of release were dashed when we were transferred to Livingstone Prison, only seven km from the border. It was June 1973, two years since we were detained in Milima Prison. Conditions in the prison were quite good, but we remembered how our fellow-fighters from Mboroma had been deported to Rhodesia and feared that the same would happen to us.

In Livingstone we had three visits from ZANU senior officials. We feared that they were trying to compensate for a lack of Western Zimbabwean fighters in ZANU and decided not to join them. We were fully aware that many of our comrades, Rex Nhongo, for example, had defected to ZANU soon after the eruption of the ZAPU crisis in 1970.

The exodus continued from that time till our detention in June 1971. In addition to Rex Nhongo, Robson Manyika (former ZPRA Chief of Staff), Thomas Nhari, Solomon Badza and others were now ZANU commanders with a high profile. Many rank and file ZPRA comrades defected to ZANU. Their departure diminished ZPRA's capability and boosted the operational capacity of ZANLA. I believe that a dramatic rise in ZANLA's effectiveness in the theatre of operation from 1972 onwards may have resulted from additional combatants from ZPRA, who brought with them a certain amount of ideological direction, military expertise and experience in field operations.

We March 11th combatants saw no future operating under ZAPU. If the ZANU visitors to Livingstone had presented a united statement of purpose, we could probably have persuaded our comrades to move into ZANLA.

I LEAVE ZAMBIA FOR THE UK

Meanwhile, in the UK, Zwelibanzi Mzilethi and my wife Ratie were advised to concentrate their efforts on trying to get me released. Ratie took the lead in demanding that her husband should join her after being detained without trial in a foreign country. One warm April day in 1974, I was released, escorted on the train to Lusaka, stayed there overnight and taken to the airport to fly to London.

I went to study at the Selly Oak Colleges in Birmingham. Meanwhile I worked with Zwelibanzi Mzilethi, my wife Ratie and Jacob Moyo to campaign for the release of the comrades in Zambia. We had help from Joan Lester, Minister of State for Foreign Affairs in the Labour government.

We also strove to find places where our colleagues could study. A few days before the Universities and Colleges opened for the academic year in 1974/5, we were informed that all the comrades were due to be released for deportation to the UK. They arrived in time to start the academic year with the other students. At the end of that year, some of us who were less keen on schooling found jobs and settled down.

Meanwhile we learned that, while the March 11 Movement seemed to be growing in the UK, the chances of its members returning to the struggle hardly brightened.

I myself did a BA Honours in Social Sciences at York University. I then went to Swansea University College in Wales from where I graduated in 1980 with a M Sc (Econ) in Social Planning.

Marieke Faber Clarke summarised Joshua Mahlathini's book at his request.

MOFFAT NDLOVU
Entered Inyathi School 1958.

I was born some time in April 1942. I went to Matshetsheni Primary School, east of Gwanda town, up to Standard Three and then went to Glass Block No 1 for my Standard 4. I proceeded to Gloag Ranch Mission for Standard 5 and then to Inyathi School from 1958-62, starting with Standard 6. At Inyathi Secondary School I completed Cambridge Overseas Certificate.

My brother was detained during the Freedom Struggle. Our village in Gwanda was attacked by the Rhodesian military. My father was carrying his great-grandchild in his arms: the bullets went through the flesh of her legs as he carried her out of the house. (This was in the early 1970's).

My desire as a young boy was to be a minister of religion in the London Missionary Society (LMS), and this wish continued till I went to Inyathi Secondary School. The school was then predominantly a boys' school. I won all the book prizes as I went through the school.

The Inyathi School principal was Mr Kenneth Maltus Smith. He was an ex-soldier and wore army boots. He was a very nice man and a very good teacher of English Language, English Literature as well as Geography. He produced a booklet on contour mapping which we students used. I am told that other schools used these as well.

I was already interested in politics. I had a photo of Joshua Nkomo placed over the bookshelf at the top of my bed. During the regular Saturday inspection, Mr Smith found this photo and asked whether Mr Nkomo was my relative. I said "Yes", which was not true. Mr Nkomo was not related to me.

In those days, it was common for students to belong to a group at school. The group that I belonged to was called the Soviets[52], because we were considered radicals. At the time, juniors (from Standard 6 to Form 2) slept on the cold cement floor. But prefects and students in Forms 3 and 4 like Aleke Banda[53] slept on beds. Aleke and I slept in the same dormitory which was named after the LMS missionary John Whiteside. But Aleke had a bed and I as a junior slept on the floor. Aleke was so intelligent that he came top in *IsiZulu* although he was from a family of Malawians.

I left Inyathi School at the end of 1962 after completing Form 4. After Inyathi School I was a temporary teacher at LMS schools for one year.

I left the country for Zambia in 1964 (which became independent on 24th October). I went straight to Lusaka and met George Silundika at the ZAPU office. I enquired about opportunities for studies and was told that there were none at the time. So I proceeded to Kitwe on the Copper Belt, and got a job as a records clerk in the Anglo-American Corporation. I joined the Kitwe ZAPU branch.

It was at that time that I met and became friends with Dumiso Dabengwa and Akim Ndlovu. Dumiso Dabengwa recruited me for training in the USSR. I resigned from my Kitwe job so I could train in the USSR in "admin" – a general title – for six months or so. I was not coerced to join the Liberation Struggle but strongly felt that the liberation of my country came first.

In the Soviet Union, part of our training involved an introduction to Marxism-Leninism, and the two political systems of Socialism and Capitalism. We were taught how Capitalism had underdeveloped

---

[52] See Joshua Mahlathini Mpofu's chapter for the Soviets at Inyathi School.
[53] See chapter on Aleke Banda in this book.

and exploited Africa.[54] Our lecturer Comrade Boris was an eloquent Communist.

I returned to Lusaka from the USSR: my group stayed at a farm outside Lusaka in a block. The former Vice President Mphoko was one of the people at that farm. He slept next to the door with an A K 47 between him and me. Our plan was that, if the Rhodesian agents grabbed him, I would go for the gun to defend ourselves. I was a pretty good shot at that time.

We were deployed to Rhodesia in October 1965, just before the Unilateral Declaration of Independence, with one other man, John Guzha. We had been informed that the coast was clear and so we boarded the train from Livingstone in Zambia. But, when the train entered Rhodesia at Victoria Falls, security personnel surrounded the train, calling out our names. We did not respond and there was no escape route. When the train came to a halt, security personnel poured into the train and subjected us all to searches. We were immediately arrested, driven to Bulawayo and from there to Salisbury, now Harare.

There must have been a spy inside ZAPU: that was why we were caught at Victoria Falls. We were tried under the Law and Order Maintenance Act and were lucky not to be hanged.[55] The Special Branch brought my father from Gwanda to get me to make a confession. Inspector Gordon Binns of the Special Branch interrogated me.

Binns was unable to get anything from me: that is why my father was brought from Gwanda. When Binns told my father why I was

---

[54] Walter Rodney, an African- Guyanan, wrote a famous book: "How Europe underdeveloped Africa" published in 1972. It is still in print and available through Google.
[55] Pathisa Nyathi notes: From about 1965, there was a very high capture rate of ZAPU cadres being infiltrated into Rhodesia. This was the genesis for the fall-out in 1971, namely the March 11th Movement. The Rhodesian Special Branch was involved in setting up the Zambian Intelligence Service when Zambia became independent in 1964.

arrested and that we wished to govern the country, my father said: "There's nothing wrong about my son's wish for our country to be ruled by black people." You could see the disappointment on Binns's face. My father was never brought back again.

I was taken to Beatrice police station just outside Salisbury, handcuffed and shackled to a ring inside a cell, while every day Inspector Binns came to question me. I was given dreadful very cold food that I'd not have given to a dog. Hungry, I had no choice but to eat that food.

When we were being interrogated, the British minister Arthur Bottomley was in this country. This may have saved us a lot of trouble as there was uncertainty about its future. African security officers were visibly unsettled.

We were locked up in Chikurubi Prison in a section called "Gonakudzingwa". At one time Robert Mugabe, the ZANU leader, was locked up in our section. He had apparently committed some breach of prison regulations. He was put on "split rations"-only half of what we were supposed to get.

Between February and May 1966, we were tried under Judge Davis at Salisbury High Court. We were defended by Enock Dumbutshena, J. McNally and Davies- a young barrister. It was a long trial and indeed recorded as the longest criminal trial in Rhodesia at the time.

We witnessed legal gymnastics for the first time. Justice Davis was a known government sympathiser, who, during the trial, said that, in his opinion, the government was legal ("de jure"). It was clear to us that we were going to be found guilty, regardless of the evidence. The only question was "What sentence would we get?"

After long and at times emotional sessions, we were sentenced to ten years in prison with hard labour, under the Law and Order Maintenance Act. We were taken to Khami Maximum Security Prison outside Bulawayo. This was the top maximum security prison in the country with single cells. I am not aware that there was any prison worse than Khami.

Our conditions suddenly changed. When we disembarked from the bus, the reception was hostile. We ran through two rows of prison warders. As we did so, we were subjected to beatings. One of our comrades, Peter Madlela, sustained a broken jaw.

We were driven to Block B which was the top security unit at Khami. I was pushed into cell 15 and the door banged after me. I stood there in the middle of this cell naked, holding my earthly possessions. These comprised a sisal mat, three old blankets, a chamber pot and a tin cup of water. How long I stood there I cannot remember, but it was a long time. This cell was to be my home for many years. It was narrow and I could touch the walls on either side. High up there was a small window with bars.

For nine months we were locked in and not allowed to speak to each other or go outside the block. We would be let out of our cells to empty our chamber pots and collect water and occasionally we were let out for a shower. It was on those occasions that we could whisper to each other when the guards were looking the other way.

The food was bad at Khami. Once we were given beans that were intended for animal feed. The smell was unusual and ZAPU prisoners boycotted the stuff. But our colleagues in ZANU would take the food in the presence of officers and then put it into open drains. When we asked the colleagues why they did this, their reply was that this was part of ZANU's policy to confront ZAPU. This was taking the policy too far, since they also were affected by the terrible food.

The doors of our cells were thick with a small peep hole for staff to look at us occasionally. It was very disconcerting to see only the eye of the officer peeping.

At night, we communicated with each other by knocking on the dividing wall between the cells. Back in my cell No 15, I would sit on two blankets with the third blanket made into some kind of decoration in front of me. I would sit there for hours at a time with my head between my arms.

The corners of the perimeter wall were structures where armed guards watched us. But there were staff who were sympathetic to ZAPU.

I was on the eastern side of the building on the ground floor. When the sun shone through the small window, I would stand up to catch the sun for a few glorious moments. I would follow the sun until it disappeared. (Emmerson Mnangagwa, president of Zimbabwe from 2018, was on the western side of the block, also on the ground floor.)

If an insect entered the cell, it would become my welcome visitor for that day. It was a welcome visitor indeed! Sometimes I would follow its movements on my knees and prevent its escape. In due course I would let it go. I would never kill it.

In those nine months, my complexion changed to very light. There were no books to read. A radio would be switched on for a short time at night.

At the end of nine months, we were let out of the building and made to sit in the sun. That direct exposure to the sun after such a long time inside the cells affected some of the men so that they fainted.

When we returned to the cells we were subjected to dehumanising bodily searches. You had to remove your clothes, which consisted of a pair of shorts and a shirt, and hand them to the prison guard who would carry out the searches. After the searches, he would throw the clothes behind him. With arms outstretched and hands open you opened your mouth wide for the guard to peep in. You had to turn round and open your buttocks to show that nothing was hidden in your anus. There was a white officer who seemed to enjoy watching us being subjected to this dehumanising search.

After a long time we were allowed to study. Through Christian Care and the Red Cross, we registered for studies. I did A. levels and passed. I registered to do LL B with London University and also passed that. I was told that I was the first prisoner to pass law exams in jail.

Studying was not easy. The prison staff searched the cells from time to time: these men would throw the books all over the place, but I continued with my studies. In due course I registered for a Master's degree in Law (LL.M) with the same university.

Eventually we were moved to Block A, and I continued with my studies. In A Block we would be let out to do some physical work such as chopping firewood, shelling maize or crushing stones.

We had to dig a big pit and crush stones at the bottom of the pit. We went down by ladder and came back the same way, regardless of the weather. One day, Desmond Lardner-Burke (Minister of Justice and Law and Order 1964-1976) visited Khami Maximum Security Jail and watched us from a distance.

One day, when we were in a big cell in Block A, there was an officer called van Wyk who used very crude language. I felt so angry that I reacted and told him that I knew what I was fighting for. I was nearly beaten to death. He fetched other officers and the whole lot of them descended on me and beat me so badly that I passed out.

I woke up in a dark cell with no windows and double doors. I don't know how long I spent in that dark cell. The officers would push the food under the door, but I could not see the plate. I had to spread my arms to find the plate of food. I would hold the plate as I ate so that I could get at the food in the darkness.

Later I appeared before the Superintendent, a Mr Nelson, and van Wyk was asked to state what had happened. He gave his version of what had happened and left out the insults he had hurled at us. I was given the opportunity to ask questions, which I did. Then Lazarus Masuku, who slept next to me, was called to give an account of what had happened. Lazarus told Nelson what I had said. Questioned about what van Wyk had said, Lazarus Masuku said he was not going to put words into the officer's mouth. That was Lazarus and his lack of integrity. I was sentenced to one month loss of remission in my original sentence. This meant that I would serve one month more after the release of my colleagues.

In 1973 I was released and given a detention order. I was taken to Gwelo Prison where I joined my old group. I continued my Master of Laws studies.

Every year there was a Detainees' Tribunal: detainees would appear before the tribunal in Salisbury for the review of their detentions. I was the only one in our group who never went to the tribunal, since I never saw the value of the tribunal. Because of my decision, the Church of England Prison Chaplain Father Spong recommended that my studies should be suspended. I did not change my position on appearing before the Detainees' Tribunal. The right to study was restored when a new Prison Chaplain, Rev. Mapondera, took over from Father Spong.

Rev Mapondera was a good man. My colleagues and I smuggled letters through him. He would give us Holy Communion on a Sunday and I carried the cups and wine. He would give us a generous sip of the wine! He would also tell us what was happening outside the prison. One day he told us that somebody had been arrested with a large cache of arms (mazvakatire). We then nicknamed him Mazvakatire.

We were treated slightly better in detention. There was no more harassment. The International Committee of the Red Cross would visit us annually to check on our conditions. The ICRC took up our grievances with the officials.

In May 1978 I was released from detention. I joined my sister's family in New Magwegwe in Bulawayo. I was feeling homesick and so I decided to go for a few days to Matshetsheni in Gwanda. The security situation was tense. What touched me most was that my relations and neighbours were more concerned about my safety than they were about theirs. That touched me deeply.

Back in Bulawayo, I stayed with my sister Queenie and her husband Abednego Sigidi, a very nice couple. But I got wind that the Special Branch was spying on me, so I relocated to Pelandaba where I stayed with the Jacob Nare family.

I knew Jacob Nare from when we were together at Inyathi Secondary School. I stayed with him and his family for some time while trying to find employment. I was unsuccessful. Finally I got a British Council scholarship to go to Swansea University College through the efforts of my young sister Mildred and her husband Strike Mkandla.[56] I am very grateful to them and to the British Council.

Armed with a British passport, I went through what was then Jan Smuts airport in South Africa. At the departure lounge, there were segregated rows for blacks and for whites. Defiantly I joined the Whites' row, though an unfortunate black guard tried to persuade me to join the Blacks' row. I stubbornly refused and proceeded to the counter where I handed my passport to a white officer. He said something in Afrikaans and I told him in no polite language that I did not speak Afrikaans. He said something like "Exkus" and stamped my passport with great vigour before throwing it at me. My consolation was that I had defeated apartheid in my small way.

The British Council met me at London Heathrow airport. My sister Mildred was also there. I stayed in London for a few days and, boy, was it cold! This was 1978.

In due course I boarded the Swansea train. In Swansea I went to Mrs Jones's house till I found alternative accommodation: they were very nice people. At Swansea University I met my old Inyathi schoolmate Joshua Mahlathini Mpofu. I enjoyed my stay in Wales and made many friends there, black and white. I was elected chairman of the

---

[56] See chapter on Mildred Mkandla nee Ndlovu

Swansea University Anti-Apartheid Movement. While I was chairman, we organised a sit-in against a South African Company, called Roberts Construction, which was trying to recruit white engineers for its operations in South Africa. We just followed them around the University until they abandoned the exercise.

I returned to Zimbabwe after the April 1980 elections, having got my M Sc. I got a job with the Ministry of Labour, in the department of Manpower Planning. I was never fully appointed as a civil servant, because my appointment was supposed to be subject to ministerial approval. The minister then was Frederick Shava. I objected to this discrimination. I was the only Ndebele at that senior level: I asked why I was subjected to this, while other officers were not. I got fed up and joined the parastatal called the Agriculture and Rural Development Authority, as Planning and Research Officer for Matabeleland.

I carried out extensive research in Matabeleland South on an appropriate resettlement model. All the three resettlement models, A, B and C, were then based on the Mashonaland environment. Matabeleland differed in rainfall patterns and in culture.

This was the time when dissidents began to make their presence felt. I thought that, to get acceptance in the region, I needed the support of Dr Joshua Nkomo, the ZAPU leader. I briefed him that I was going to do research on land resettlement Model D in Matabeleland. He gave me his full support. Josh (Umdala) always supported development initiatives. This research project was funded by the United Nations Development Programme. A UNDP consultant worked with me.

After the research was finished, the consultant and I submitted the conclusions to the Ministry of Lands. Dr Chitsike, the Permanent Secretary to Minister Sidney Sekeramayi, liked my paper and we presented the research paper on Model D based on grazing.

During the lunch that Dr Chitsike provided, he said he wondered how I carried out that successful research in an area infested with dissidents. I read that to mean that he considered me a dissident or sympathiser, which I was not. I think the community protected me.

However, the ministry was reluctant to implement Model D and continued to implement Models A, B and C. These models were unsuitable for Matabeleland South because the area has too little rain.

I resigned from ARDA: I could not implement resettlement models that did not address the felt needs of the local people, taking into consideration the geography of the area. The UNDP consultant tried to persuade me to stay, but I could not do something that I knew was not good for the people of Matabeleland South simply to retain my job. So in 1983 I joined Bulawayo City Council and worked there till 2007. I rose through the ranks till I became clerk and retired in April 2007.

MY PRIVATE LIFE

I married in 1985: my wife and I have two sons. She is ZAPU but not very active. I am also a member of ZAPU and I am still in the United Congregational Church of Southern Africa, the successor body to the London Missionary Society.

After retirement I went to Namibia to do capacity-building. It was a good experience. It was a nice country. The level of tolerance in politics was something new to me. Here was a new nation that tolerated opposition. Namibia was fresh air to me.

I am a pensioner now and struggle to survive. The national revolution has devoured its children. I think that the ideals we fought so hard for, and for which we suffered so much, have been trashed by the government since 1980. Cry the beloved country!

Interview by Marieke Faber Clarke at Bulawayo.

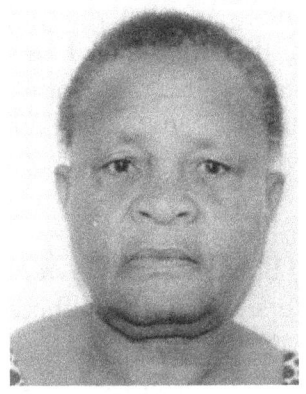

MILDRED MKANDLA
(nee Ndlovu)
She entered Inyathi School in 1960

I was born on 12 March 1946 at Matshetheni under Chief Mzimuni Masuku. My parents were Nsuku and Silina Tshuma. Nsuku's father was Mishi and his mother Gege Mpala. Njeleza was Mishi's son. I was the last born in a family of six children: two boys, Misheck and Moffat, and four girls, Melody, Lizzie, Queenie and myself.

I had a traditional round hut called Enxiweni. The modern houses were rectangular and built out of brick. I still remember my bed in the round hut: it was made of skin strips woven on a wooden frame. I will not forget the day when black ants bit me. Gogo (Granny) NakaEva had a big round hut. My grandfather was a polygamous man who used frequently to slaughter cattle for his big family. Our father used to get a leg to eat whenever a beast was slaughtered. Both my parents were church members.

Our local school, Matshetsheni Primary School, belonged to the London Missionary Society (LMS) and there I started Sub-Standard A in 1954. I remember a few of the teachers at the school: Amos Mutswakayi Sibanda, Mr Sigola my first teacher, Lazarus Khumalo, Nathaniel Ngwenya, Hastings Chawuluka, Queenie Ndlovu, Ellen Moyo, Lizzie Ncube and Ellen Ndlovu.

I did Sub-Standards A and B in the same year, 1957. This was because I had had a good head start: in our kitchen hut there was a blackboard that my brother Moffat[57] used when teaching me. I attended Matshetsheni Primary School up to Standard 3.

---

[57] See chapter on Moffat Ndlovu

In 1958 I went to do Standard 4 at Hope Fountain Mission, another LMS institution nearer Bulawayo. I was there till 1959 when I was doing Standard 5. I went to a boarding school because my mother passed on when I was ten years of age. My father valued education, which was not the case with his friends, who were not keen to educate girl children.

In 1960, I proceeded to Inyathi Mission to do Standard 6. We were the first and last Standard 6 group to be boarders. In our group there were three girls from Hope Fountain and two boys, Zephaniah Ndlovu and Sipho Tshuma. Prior to our arrival at Inyathi Mission, boarding facilities were reserved for boys and girls at secondary school level.

The Principal at Inyathi Mission was Ken Maltus Smith. Other teachers at the school were Elijah Mdluli and Joel Ndlovu. Both my brothers Misheck and Moffat attended Inyathi Mission. I remember, in 1959, going from Hope Fountain Mission to attend centenary celebrations at Inyathi Mission. Inyathi Mission was opened in December 1859. I still have a vivid memory of ox-wagons that were part of the celebrations.

Both my brothers were politically minded. I remember some of the books that they used to read. There was "Pilgrim's Progress" by John Bunyan and "Zambia Shall be Free" by Kenneth Kaunda.

We were exposed to racial injustice at a tender age. We used to go to Colleen Bawn[58] to sell fresh farm produce. We could not help seeing discrimination perpetrated against us blacks. We also experienced the cruel evictions of the Hadane people who were coming from near Esigodini. It was about 1952 or 1953 and I was six years of age at the time. The evictees were housed in makeshift accommodation on a rainy day. I remember my mother bringing along Beniya Agnes

---

[58] Colleen Bawn is a small settlement where cement is mined and from where it is taken to Bulawayo's Cement Siding to be processed. Colleen Bawn is South of Gwanda and near Ematshetsheni, where Moffat and Mildred Ndlovu grew up.

Moyo, whom, dripping wet, she tucked in my blankets. She and I later became friends.

In 1960 my brother Misheck fell out of favour with white authorities at the school. He was expelled and asked to go away that very same day in the evening. I left him at Badala on the Nkayi-Bulawayo Road. It was James Kamanga who suggested, "I think we had better act." Mnyama was Head boy at the time.

The whole school flocked to Badala in solidarity with Misheck. We found and brought him back to school. We argued that he should not have been sent away at night. When we came back, James Mhlanga, the Farm Manager, took me into his car. I was the smallest girl among the student body.

In the morning of the following day, Misheck, who was doing Form 2, left Inyathi Mission. He later found work with the Rhodesia Omnibus Company (ROC). There he would not accept a white boss. When he was studying with the Central African Correspondence College, he got sight of a signature of one Mr Dupont[59] on tutorial material. He immediately threw away that material. Aleke Banda was ahead of us at Inyathi School.[60] We had Noble Chituta.

Both my brothers were arrested and detained; Misheck at Wha Wha Prison and Moffat at Khami Prison. That broke our father's heart, to the point where he began to drink a lot of *mahewu*, a traditional non-intoxicating brew. My brothers were beaten and tortured.

At Inyathi Mission, I stayed up to Form 2, after which I proceeded to the Salvation Army's Usher Institute near Figtree. My mother had always wanted me to do either Domestic Science or Nursing. I wanted to be an engineer. Sadly, my mother died before I could achieve either of her dreams. It was out of the desire to fulfil my

---

[59] Clifford Dupont was Minister of Justice, Law and Order under Ian Smith's Rhodesia Front "Government" which declared Unilateral Independence from the United Kingdom in 1965.
[60] See Chapter on Aleke Banda.

mother's wish that I went to do Domestic Science where Major Gardner was Head of Usher Institute. So, I was at Usher Institute from 1963 to 1965.

I went back to Inyathi Mission, this time as a teacher in the secondary section of the school. I was under Mrs Smith in the Domestic Science Department. That was from 1965 to 1966. At the time, Moffat was at Khami Prison. In 1967 I transferred to Hope Fountain where I spent two years. Mr S. P. Ndlovu was Principal. Meanwhile, I did "O" and "A" Levels through correspondence. Then I was academically qualified to do nurse training at Mpilo Government Hospital. This was in line with my mother's second wish.

During my days at Hope Fountain, I was riled by racism that was practised on the Rhodesia Omnibus Company (ROC) buses. At the very entrance of the bus there was a note directed at white passengers: "Move to the rear the driver stinks." I found myself advising black passengers to distribute themselves everywhere in the bus in defiance of the racial segregation that was taking place during those colonial days.

From 1969 to 1972 I trained as a nurse at Mpilo Hospital in Bulawayo, where I qualified as a State Registered Nurse (SRN). Still at Mpilo, I went on to do midwifery and obtained a State Certified Midwifery (SCM) certificate, Zimbabwe. Between 1973 and 1974 I worked at Mpilo's Wards C1, C3 and B6. Then it was time to pack my bags and go overseas.

In 1974 I went to Scotland, where I did a short course in intensive care nursing. At the Yeoville District Hospital in Somerset I did Midwifery for six months, training under the auspices of the Midwives Board of England: this qualified me to practise in the United Kingdom and I worked there as a midwife for a short time in 1976. That year, on 14th August, I married Strike Mkandla[61]. We

---

[61] Dr Strike Mkandla has over 20 years' experience in policy development, analysis and presentation.

have three children: Nozikhali Lindile, a daughter (1977); Ndabayezwe Andile, a boy (1980) and Nonhlanhla Phangisile, another daughter (1985).

As part of my efforts to advance myself academically, I did a Diploma and a Bachelor of Arts (BA) in Applied Social Studies. I went on to do a Master's degree in Health Education, and a PhD in Social Psychology.

When my husband Strike went to Zambia, where he worked for the United Nations Institute for Namibia[62], the family relocated with him. At the end of 1990, we went back to Zimbabwe. It was ironic that our children, whose names were Nguni, did IsiNdebele as a second language. We lived in Zimbabwe between 1991 and 1992. In 1993 we set off for Nairobi. My husband worked till his retirement in 2010 in Kenya and Ethiopia for the United Nations Environment Programme.

Interview by Pathisa Nyathi

---

[62] Strike Mkandla was head of Information and Documentation at the United Nations Institute for Namibia 1985-1990.

JACK P. NHLIZIYO
Probably entered Inyathi School in 1961
Head boy at Inyathi School in 1964

District administrator for Bubi, Nkayi and Tsholotsho districts after 1980

This interview by Marieke Clarke and Kudzai Chikomo took place at Bulawayo, 2012.

HOW MY FAMILY CAME TO BE EVICTED
Nhliziyo: My family were evicted from Filabusi to the Shangani Reserve in 1952. It was the eighth time that we had been moved since the Conquest. Many other students at Inyathi School had also been evicted from their earlier homes. When my family were evicted to Shangani, others were evicted to Tsholotsho, for instance. Some of us students were being resettled for the third time, not because they and their households wanted to move, but because the white authorities were always moving them from one place to another.

I remember a time, long before the 1952 evictions, when we were moved from the Malole area to a place called Singwango under a chief Sibasa. And we were moved back to the other side of the river Malonge, near Wanezi mission, and were promised we were going to be there a long time. We were promised that we wouldn't be moved any more. Then in 1952 we were evicted forcibly. There were soldiers and police involved. The whole thing was done in a very cruel way. For instance my home was destroyed at midnight.

Kuzai Chikomo: So there was no warning?

Nhliziyo: There was no notice. The officials told everyone to leave. And people were just in their houses, only to hear they were being evicted.

I remember a neighbour being evicted a day or two before our home was evicted. We moved in the direction of the neighbours to see what was happening. As we were hiding behind rocks, a couple of soldiers looked in our direction and we got frightened and ran away, not knowing that the soldiers would be coming for our home as well.

Then a few days later, at midnight, soldiers came in trucks to carry our belongings away without warning or even giving us time to pack.

It was before dawn when we were being taken through Bulawayo to a place we didn't know. What we did know is that we went through Nkayi, then to Gwelutshena, and we must have arrived at Gwelutshena at about midday the following day.

We spent the whole day not knowing what was happening or what to do. There was a borehole: we didn't know what a borehole was, only to learn it was for collection of water. We were only yet to discover that there were many families placed around this borehole.

We were told this small machine is a borehole: the borehole was what we were to use to supply us with water. Then we started pumping.

The next day the agricultural extension officers came to show my parents where the fields were supposed to be and where the homes were supposed to be. After being shown that, we started work. We started clearing and cutting away. This happened around September/ October: I remember this because it was about to rain.

We built the homes: some people had one hut, others had two, depending on how strong the people were and able to build.
We organised things, working together, so that one household would be building a hut on one day. The next day we would build another hut for another household, until we ended up with about three to four huts for each family.

Then came the task of clearing the fields. This took a long time. This was the difficult part: clearing huge trees, clearing the land for tillage. And our cattle had died already: most of the cattle had died as a result of disease and from eating a poisonous plant.

I was about 13 years old at the time. Our elder brothers accompanied the cattle on the train. Once the cattle had been driven off the train, the bigger boys would separate out the cattle according to the different families, and then they started driving them.

The white authorities could have decided that our cattle were to be driven to Kwekwe, which was closer to our old homes. But instead, the cattle were taken by train to Gwayi. This place was full of the poisonous herb *umkhawuzane.* So, as soon as the cattle were let out of the train, they started to eat the first green thing they saw, and it was poisonous! We lost a lot of livestock; cattle, goats, sheep, donkeys, everything! It was a great loss. Life was very painful as there was no compensation for the loss of the animals that just died and were left lying on the ground. Life was difficult trying to get used to a new life as we didn't have oxen.

We didn't know where the school was, or where the shops were. We were just in the bush. There was no sign of civilisation, not even a bus stop. We were just lost: we didn't know where to start.

Bit by bit we learned where there was a school, where the stores were, and then we started acclimatising and getting used to the situation.

We were told we were being evicted because the white government of the time was compensating white British soldiers who had fought in the Second World War. The Rhodesian government was giving these British ex-servicemen land (on the watershed where amaNdebele people had earlier settled. MFC). Some black Rhodesian men had fought in the Second World War supporting the British Forces, but the former black soldiers who had fought were given useless things, like bicycles, instead of land.

The former black soldiers knew what was wrong with the places to which they were being sent: the places were called *emaguswini* which means, in the bushes. The type of grass there was not good and the poisonous plant *umkhawuzane* was rampant.

Before the evictions, our elders used to have meetings. Our fathers paid a lot of money to lawyers to try to stop us being evicted.[63]

THE RESULTS OF THE EVICTIONS

JN: Many things were disturbed. Some young people lost their education, as they were displaced from their schools and did not go to school in the year of the eviction. Those students who eventually went back to school had to repeat the standards that they had passed or had done the previous year.

KC: When you moved to the new school, how was it? Was it easy to adjust, did you find the subjects easy?

JN: It was not difficult, since we had previously done the work. I had just completed Standard 1.When I moved to the new school, I had to repeat Standard 1. We had to get used to the new environment and that took a bit of time.

KC: Were you paying the school fees?

JN: Our parents had to pay and that means that they had to pay again the following year for the repeated standards.

KC: So you repeated the same standard at Nkayi?

JN: Yes.

KC: How did you proceed from there?

JN: Well, I went as far as Standard 6 at Nkayi.

---

[63] See Bhebe, Ngwabi: "Benjamin Burombo" (The College Press, Harare, 1989)

HOW I CAME TO INYATHI SCHOOL

KC: I'd like to know how you came to Inyathi School so I can get an idea of the kind of relationship you had with Marieke.

JN: I went to Inyathi for my secondary education and that's when I met Marieke.

KC: Marieke was a teacher then?

JN: Yes. She had come to teach at Inyathi in September 1963.

KC: What subjects was she teaching?

JN: She was teaching History, English Language, English Literature and Latin.[64] Marieke was a great teacher, if there was something that we did not understand, we would go to her house and she would assist us. She was like a sister to us.

KC: And this was now secondary school. Did you have any memorable experiences?
JN: There weren't many except that the (Liberation) Struggle was still on in the 1960's. Any white person who was friendly to Africans was not liked by the then Government and that's how Marieke was deported.

KC: How close was Marieke to Africans?

JN: She was generally friendly: she was one of the teachers we liked.

KC: Were there any particular events during that time that would make you remember Marieke?

JN: When in November 1964 she got deported by the government of the time, I was one of the students who accompanied her to the airport.

---

[64] MC made some clarifications here.

KC: And were you aware of what was happening?

JN: Yes, we knew what was happening, that the government of the time had deported her and that they did not want white people to be friendly to Africans.

KC: How did she cope with having to avoid the police while yet being friendly to Africans?

JN: She took people as people and did not see colour. Most white people in Rhodesia at that time did not see things that way.

KC: Where could the instruction have come from for her to be deported? Was it from Salisbury or internal agents in Inyathi?

JN: Government had its own way of working. If you were discovered to be on the wrong side, the government did not hesitate to deal with you.

LETTER FROM JACK NHLIZIYO TO MARIEKE CLARKE AFTER HER DEPORTATION

Goromonzi Secondary School
Salisbury
11th June, 1965

"All hope is gone and there are no more memories left with you of the boy who left with you from the hall (at Inyathi School) where we had a film show and was bidding you a happy farewell and desirous to know your future plans. I hope you are just wondering what befell the class that you left on the eve of the examinations[65]. And at the same time you are wondering what has come of some of those who used to be your close friends among the Form 4 and of course I am among those."

---

[65] The Inyathi School students in Forms 2 and 4, which Marieke taught, were due to sit Junior Certificate and Cambridge Certificate examinations at the end of the term, only a couple of weeks after Marieke was deported.

A BREAK IN THE FRIENDSHIP
JN: There was a break in the friendship between Marieke and me. Even after Independence, Marieke could not return to Inyathi. It was only after Gukurahundi was over and the Unity Accord had been sealed in 1987, that we were able to communicate freely again.

MARIEKE RETURNS TO INYATHI IN 1989
Now Mr Nhliziyo was District Administrator of Bubi District, whose headquarters was at the government camp a few hundred metres from Inyathi School.
KC: And so you met again?

JN: And we still were friends. Because I knew that the break in our communication was not intended.

JN: When she returned, as I was District Administrator at Inyathi and a former student of Marieke's, I was very interested to show her things in my District that she wanted to see. I was also interested in showing her what I liked to do as DA. At the same time I knew she was interested in places of historical importance, so I showed her places that had some historical background. I showed her where King Lobhengula lived and where his ministers lived. One of them is the site where Queen Lozikeyi Dlodlo was buried. When we got to the queen's grave, her brother Mazha Dlodlo [66] had just died. And he had also been buried near his sister's grave.

J. ZWELIBANZI MZILETHI WROTE:
J.P. Nhliziyo was my senior at school and also at home at Nkayi. The longest time I lived in close contact with him was when we were at Inyathi School, where he was my prefect and a brother to me. He was a very respected member of the Inyathi School community. A curious thing was that he never showed political leanings, but he turned a blind eye and let us get away with a lot of issues which could have led to my being severely punished or expelled from the

---

[66] Mazha Dlodlo was the father-in-law of Welshman Mabhena. See Chapter on Welshman Mabhena

school. We knew it was his role to make us stay studying at school rather than to be expelled.

At Inyathi he acted as an advisor to most of us, and particularly to boys from Nkayi. If we were in trouble, I would personally rush to him knowing that even the school staff trusted him in most issues. He would behave in a very tough manner, but he would not hand me to the authorities for punishment. He would instead let me dig in the garden as light punishment and turn a blind eye to most issues leading to serious problems in the Shangani Advancing Students' Association. He was a key member of SASA. At one point some of us wanted to break away from SASA and start a new organisation, when we felt that the leadership was not as radical as we wanted it to be. He refused to let us do that. He was so respected that we felt we had to follow his advice and we abandoned our plan.

My ally was Amon Mankebe Sibanda and we two had to tell our followers that our advisers had recommended not to make the move. It is strange how we all listened to Nhliziyo's advice and took it seriously. Nobody would challenge what he had said.

When I was appointed Provincial Administrator for Matabeleland North, the Province did not have credible leadership in the form of district administrators. I specifically requested the Public Service Commission (PSC) to give me experienced people.

Mr Thompson, the then PSC chairman, with other commissioners, asked me to identify potential candidates to be district administrators. With the Commission's agreement I went to Nhliziyo. He was the senior clerk and, after I had talked to him, he gave me a couple of names and to my surprise he left himself out. I guess he assumed I would include him in the group. I did include him as a key person, and he agreed, of course. I identified altogether six administrators who I knew were very credible.

Nhliziyo had a lot of experience in local government affairs: he became one of the key senior persons that I had as district administrators in Matabeleland North. He was very instrumental in helping to end the Civil War in the province. He never left Nkayi even during the worst period. Indeed he was a key advisor to me as Provincial Administrator, as he had been at school. He was very cool-headed and never dealt with issues emotionally. Nhliziyo made my job as Provincial Administrator very light.

For more information on the background to Jack Nhliziyo's life, see Violence and Memory (Alexander, Jocelyn; McGregor, JoAnn and Ranger, Terence: published James Currey, Oxford 2000). Nhliziyo himself said to MFC: "This book is the story of my life".

Jack P Nhliziyo passed away on 28th April 2018. Pathisa Nyathi attended his funeral representing also Marieke.

Marieke Clarke adds: When I returned to Zimbabwe in 1989, Mr Mzilethi as provincial administrator said I could not go to Nkayi, as it was still unsafe. (See chapter about J. Z. Mzilethi for the military background to Mr Nhliziyo's achievement in containing the "dissidents" at Nkayi.) In 1991 I did go to Nkayi and talked to the co-operators at Nkayi, the so-called ex dissidents. What struck me most forcibly about Isifiso Sikazulu Collective Co-operative was their extremely poor command of English. These young soldiers had lost so much by fighting for their country.

Rehabilitation of former dissidents at Nkayi

JOBURG ZWELIBANZI MZILETHI
Entered Inyathi School in 1963.

ZPRA combatant
Provincial Administrator in independent Zimbabwe

My family was not in the struggle. They were London Missionary Society people. My grandfather's name was Mgwahu Madida. He came with Tshabalala and Nxumalo from Swaziland and had lots of cattle. We had first settled in Gazaland, and then crossed into Lobhengula's territory. The family settled near Nungwa Mountain in Bubi District and finally reached Inyathi. King Mzilikazi named my grandfather Mzilethi, "One who brings himself," because he voluntarily joined Ndebele society.

Grandfather had many wives, so he could no longer be a LMS minister and seems to have become an Anglican lay preacher, which he was till he died quite young. He experienced heart seizure while within the church. My grandfather is buried at Inyathi behind Ndumba Hill. He never paid any attention to white guys.

My grandmother witnessed the 1893 Anglo-Ndebele War (Imfazo I). She was in the Ndebele contingent that followed the king as he fled to Pupu across the Shangani River. When Grandfather died, most of his wives disappeared. But my grandmother, who was a very strong woman, stayed at Grandfather's homestead and had a child by a Moyo man known as Mayelane. Mayelane was one of the *imbovane*[67] men who stayed at King Lobhengula's royal town. My grandmother had one daughter and four or five sons.

These descendants of my grandfather and grandmother were the people with whom we went to Shangani. Quite a number of people from our neighbourhood went. We travelled on foot, but with scotch carts.

---

[67] Captives trained to serve the king.

For in 1942 the whole area in Bubi District where we lived was being portioned out to be available for white British men who were fighting in World War II (1939-45), and so we had to move to Nkayi. People who refused to move were violently treated.

I was the second son of the eldest son of my grandparents. My father was just a farmer. My own mother died in childbirth. She was a follower of the LMS and a member of their women's movement. I was brought up my grandmother.

The chieftainship (that of Sijeza Masuku) was also abolished and we were moved to the chieftainship of Tshugulu Tshabalala. For some reason we found ourselves in the chieftainship of Malisa over the Shangani River (in Kwekwe District). But we were Chief Tshugulu's people, and after living under Malisa Moyo in Silobela, Kwekwe District, for a couple of years we moved back across the Shangani River at Nkayi to be with our own chief.

EDUCATION

I went to primary school at Nkayi and Zenka Mission. I did the first few months of secondary school at John Tallach School at Ingwenya Mission of the Free Presbyterian Church of Scotland. But my brother, who was teaching there, had some misunderstanding with the missionaries and I left John Tallach School.

I then went to Inyathi Secondary School. My father paid the school fees in cash. Some students whose parents could not pay cash would pay the fees in kind: for instance, the parents would bring bags of sorghum grain in lieu of cash.

Inyathi prepared us much better for the outside world than other schools did. The other schools wanted you to remain dumb and deaf. At Ingwenya Mission, there had been no Debating Society and instead there was Catechism.

The progressive atmosphere at Inyathi was probably due to the headmaster of our time, Kenneth Maltus Smith. He touched me in a way that made you realise that you were being prepared for the outside world. Also Inyathi School was well equipped with books by people like Kwame Nkrumah of Ghana. Other schools would have removed such books.

Miss Jenny Bryson taught us about World War II[68] which led to our interest in (John Buchan's book) "The 39 Steps" and the Black Stones Group. (See below). Only Inyathi could provide that.

A student's thoughts about his teacher and friend

> *I should like to stress that Marieke Clarke was unique when compared to other white teachers at Inyathi. She not only related well to the students but also with the outside community as well. She was seen mingling with the outside community while donning some headgear, as did Ndebele women in the community.*
>
> *The way Marieke was deported had a lasting effect on the students, particularly those who were inclined towards nationalism. They arrived at the conclusion that the regime was not just racist, but wished to entrench an evil and repressive system. One student even remarked that the regime must be fought and defeated at all costs. This particular student, however, did not join the Liberation Struggle. Some students travelled in another car as far as the airport to accompany the teacher that they loved dearly.*
> **Marieke reflects**: *Zweli Mzilethi tried to prevent my deportation, which I think he thought was likely. He came to my home and asked me to take on a role, perhaps as senior member, for the Student Christian Movement so that the Rhodesian authorities would think I was more respectable than I really was. I told him the truth, which was that I was too busy. The police came soon afterwards.*
>
> *As I was being taken away, Zweli and his colleagues in the Invisible Black Stones organised a guard of honour. This supported me as I was driven by the police out of the school premises to Bulawayo.*

---

[68] This was apparently in the Junior Certificate syllabus (MC)

EARLY POLITICAL ACTIVITIES
Ken Smith and the boarding master Mr Masola used to watch us students eating every day. Once there was a big strike. In those early days I was doing rebellious things which would not be classified as political.

Later, but as a young boy, I went round Shangani with Welshman Mabhena (a relative of mine) on the back of his scooter.[69] I must admit that, at first, the scooter was the attraction, and I did not see how seriously he was working as I travelled with him. My first involvement was when the District Commissioner was insulting old people: I threw myself into opposing him.

A group of us founded the Shangani Advancing Students' Association while we were at Inyathi. Apart from me, the members included Amon Mankebe Sibanda, Jack Nhliziyo and Joshua Mahlathini Mpofu. SASA looked at the development of the whole of the Shangani Reserve. We wanted to develop the area, conscientize the youth and put in demands. We wanted good roads, secondary schools and general infra- structure at Shangani. SASA also had women members. Gina Ncube (now Mrs Madlela) was probably a member. SASA functioned in the holidays as well as in term time.

From reading "The 39 Steps" by John Buchan, we founded the Black Stones, which was a secret organisation and only for people of courage. Lenie Msimanga was one of the girl members. We were doing rebellious and very silly things like cutting water pipes. Black Stones would beat up people if their football team lost a match.

VISITING PEOPLE IN BUBI DISTRICT OUTSIDE THE SCHOOL
The events of 1893 had become folklore. Many ex combatants from Lobhengula's defeated army had settled down in Bubi District near Inyathi School. We had old people who had fought in that war. (But there was no place in an *ibutho* for a seriously wounded soldier, so none of our informants would have been seriously injured. A soldier

---

[69] For more about this time, see Clarke and Nyathi "Welshman Hadane Mabhena" (Amagugu, Bulawayo, 2010)

who was badly wounded would beg his comrades to kill him). Some of these men still wore *amabhetshu*.[70] We would go at weekends to talk to people like Cain Mathema, who had fought, and the *imbongi*[71] Ginyilitshe Hlabangana etc. We knew all these old people and would ask what happened in 1893. (We should have recorded it). There were people like grandparents who would say "You must not sing these songs till the king comes again." They were referring to the Inxwala song. (The Inxwala ceremony formed the apex of Ndebele religion. MFC)

We got the contacts bcause most of us, who were from Shangani or Kezi, had relatives living locally, Buses came at 3 to take people to the city. Others would stay locally and then go home later. The Khabos and the Bhebhes were living at Inyathi, of course. Our uncles and other family members were at Lupane. Other family members came from Fort Rixon.

GETTING IN TOUCH WITH THE LIBERATION MOVEMENT
I took Junior Certificate in 1964 but left school before I did Cambridge Certificate[72]. We were already at school in touch with the Liberation Movement through Welshman Mabhena, because he never stopped (work for the Movement). There were very few primary school teachers at Shangani who were not working with him in the Freedom Movement. Mabhena was a true nationalist who wanted to represent the people who had sent him.

We left Matabeleland underground, but the idea was to come back to Matabeleland and liberate our country. I taught briefly at Enyandeni near Matobo Research Station. Things became impossible, as I had been arrested and spent time at most police stations. I was charged with being trained in North Korea! Justice J. R. Dendy Young got me off. Just down from the court, I was taken to Gweru police station and treated quite well. I went on hunger strike and began to swell up and was hospitalised. Then I escaped.

---

[70] Traditional men's lower garment
[71] Praise singer
[72] I did Cambridge Certificate privately later.

There were people who organised all these sorts of things which even reached me in hospital. I was cuffed to the bed, but a nurse came and told me that arrangements had been made for me to leave.

"When you go to the toilet," she said, "The window will be open. Go over the fence at the back." A boy watching over me removed the cuffs and that was the signal. I had to escape wearing prison clothes. A vehicle was waiting for me and I was taken to Nkayi and then on to Bulawayo. I was joined by others who had been in detention and went underground. Thenjiwe Lesabe organised all this.

The following morning, the radios said that police were looking for armed men. I had been put in a house in Mpopoma and the detectives came in. The housewife said that Mzilethi was her peasant uncle. They asked her to leave her shoes and when she left, I put on her shoes and gown. I also changed my facial appearance. I went to the outside toilet and took off towards Khami.

The police did not start looking for me for 30 minutes. I spent the daylight hours in the bush for one month till Lesabe turned up. Taffy Moyo had given the vehicle. I went to the contact person, who took me to another place, following Glenville, on the Victoria Falls Road. I was put in the house of a white man who worked for Premier Radios. But he had a worker who was known to be an informer. The vehicle took the informer away.

The white man warned me. I was told I must move away and, as I went into the bush, I could see cars coming. I feared the police dogs. I managed to leave and got into a bus going to Pumula, where Lenie Msimanga was living. She signalled "Keep out!" I went to Lesabe, who said she was planning to move me that night. My group of combatants was moved to live in the mountains near a Bhebhe household on a farm, and from there vehicles collected us to take us to Botswana. I was then ill. For about a month I was in the 1966/7

ZAPU force. I was deployed to Sipolilo[73] as well as to Victoria Falls and Kariba.

I owe my life to Lesabe. She did her best for us. The police must have believed that I was trained. In Francistown we went to the police and made everything clear. Matante, the Botswana opposition leader, had told Khama.
(MFC: *Botswana had achieved independence in September 1966. The country's first president, from 1966 to 1980, was Seretse Khama*).

Seretse Khama sent his personal assistant and they told him that the four of us had to go to Lusaka with ANC cadres. But the aeroplane we were supposed to use blew up before we even got to it.

Peter Mackay[74] arrived with a car and a few South African women. He drove us from Francistown in Botswana, on the west side of the Hwange Game Reserve up to the Kazungula border post at the frontier with Zambia. We left, probably on 30th June, and went to the Lusaka camps.

I studied at the Moscow Military Academy and became a ZPRA leader. I reached the rank of Unit Commander (equivalent to Lieut-Colonel in the British army).

Our first operation was at Sidobe in Victoria Falls. Our ZPRA forces were already fighting alongside ANC South African forces. We were crossing by small boats which could close the waterways. We had installed an anti-aircraft gun, but the commanders realised that those who were doing the work were undertrained and I, on the other hand, could train people. Some other colleagues and I then went back to Botswana and thence to Lusaka.

I was in hospital in Moscow in 1967/8 with a serious injury following a near-fatal accident and that was the end of my military career.

---

[73] Now Guruve
[74] See Appendix on Peter Mackay at the end of this book.

I was in the March 11th Movement, which came into being in 1971 when the external wing of ZAPU splintered into three parties. We had come to the conclusion that, either all the ZPRA leaders in Zambia were informers or that there was an informer among them. How could you put untrained colleagues in charge of setting up an anti-aircraft gun? The leaders were George Nyandoro, Edward Ndlovu, J. Z. Moyo, J. Chikerema, Dumiso Dabengwa, Akim Ndlovu. We tied them up and put them in a camp. [75]

I reached the rank of Political Commissar. I was sent to the UK where I did a Joint Honours Law degree in Administration and Sociology at Hull. Then I obtained a Master's Degree in Southern African Studies. Then I went to Brown University, Providence, Rhode Island, USA where I did my Master's Degree in Demography with Rural Development as a minor subject.

I taught at Chancellor's Secondary School, Brookman's Park, near Hatfield in the UK. I returned to Zimbabwe in 1980, becoming District Administrator of Binga in Matabeleland North. I was then transferred to the Central Statistical Office in Harare, working very well with Bernard Chidzero.

In 1985 I became Provincial Administrator of Matabeleland North. One hundred dissidents surrendered to me as I pioneered development work in that province. The dissidents then set up the Isifiso sikaZulu co-operative. (See also Jack Nhliziyo's chapter).

From 1992 to 1994, I worked under Welshman Mabhena when he was Governor of Matabeleland North. In 1994, when South Africa came under democratic rule, I was transferred to become Provincial Administrator of Matabeleland South. My final posting was in Harare before I retired in 2001.

Marieke Clarke, who thinks Mzilethi is too modest, adds: Nkayi in Matabeleland North was a hotbed of resistance to white rule when I

---

[75] See the chapters by Walter Mthimkhulu and Joshua Mahlathini Mpofu.

taught at Inyathi School. Nkayi was a battlefield during the War of Liberation and the last area of Northern Matabeleland to become peaceful after the 1987 Unity Accord. All the Northern Matabeleland so-called dissidents lived there when I visited in 1993. These men surrendered to Provincial Administrator Mzilethi in extremely good physical shape and very heavily armed, so they must have been supported by local people. These so-called "dissidents" could not be defeated by a whole Brigade. [76]

Marieke Clarke interviewed J Z Mzilethi at Bulawayo 2nd October 2016 and talked on many other occasions, especially when she stayed at his home with him and his family.

---

[76] A Brigade has around 6000 soldiers (Google)

NEWMAN NDLOVU
He entered Inyathi School in 1963.

We come from the Ndlovu family. My parents say that my great-grandfather, Mahawuhawu,[77] alone, a labourer without cattle, originated in Bobonong in what is now Botswana. Because of the wars, my family moved to the then Rhodesia and integrated with the Bango families. Most of my clan originated from there. My great grandfather married into the Nkomo clan.

Thereafter my grandfather was given the name Mpotha. Mpotha married into the Bango clan and my father was given the name Sikhonkwani, which means a peg, as in a tent peg. My father was a very strong man. He worked hard and was therefore much liked. So he married a Bango daughter.

My father also had a brother called Mapholisa. My father and his brother stayed near Plumtree at a place called Silonkwe, but still under Chief Bango. They were nephews of the Bango family. My father, Sikhonkwani, popularly known as Ncwazini, was asked by his parents to stay with the in-laws because Mpotha had not paid the full lobola. It was helpful to me that my father stayed with the chief's family.

My father was married monogamously to Nami Ncube. Her family also came from what is now Botswana. She was born about 1914. The Bangos paid the lobola for my father's marriage with Nami. They had a civil marriage in May 1929.

---

[77] This means "a shield"

My father had to build his own home among the Ndlovu clan.
The first child of my father and Nami was a girl called Cecilia, the patron saint of music. The second born was a son, Zebulon, born in 1932. I was the third born, in 1944. The long gap between the children probably happened because my father was working in the diamond mines in South West Africa.

By the time I was born, the white settlers had already moved our family from Silonkwe near Plumtree to the Matopos area. We were moved to Marinoha. That is where I was born.

I started Sub A at Marinoha School and completed Standard 3 at the same school. I then went to Inyashongwe School near Maphisa, where I did Standards 4 and 5. I did Standard 6 at Marinoha in 1962. These were all LMS schools under Tshimali Mission. Then in 1963 I went to Inyathi. So in 1964 I was in Form 2 and met Marieke Clarke.

I had to leave Inyathi School after Form 2 because my brother joined the Liberation Struggle and there was no money to pay my school fees.
While I was at Inyathi, I was in the Black Stone Group.[78] This organisation was a spearhead to persuade young people to take up arms. We organised underground meetings.

My father was probably in the Struggle, too, because he and his comrades were facilitating people leaving the country. He was very angry about being moved and wanted to return to Silonkwe: "The land where we are is very barren. We can hardly farm or rear cattle."

---

[78] See also J Z Mzilethi's chapter

I left school and looked for a job. In 1966, I moved permanently to Bulawayo where I met Howard Nyathi, J. Z. Mzilethi and Jabulani among others who were seriously interested in the Struggle. We formed a group to spearhead the ZAPU struggle. Jabulani and Mzilethi crossed the Zambesi and went to join the fighters.

We remained vigilant within the party till the Lancaster House Conference (which led to Zimbabwe's gaining Independence.) I felt more optimistic that things had developed positively in the Liberation Struggle. The nationalists gained power in 1980 with the belief that the country had been handed back to the rightful owners. But, as a ZAPU party member, I was disappointed that we did not win the elections and so things did not go the way we should have loved.

We have been very badly let down by the British Government. We wanted ZAPU and ZANU to fight the elections as a united front. (Because ZANU won the elections), Matabeleland has not been developed. The men in power are filling their own pockets.

THE ATTRACTIONS OF THE ROMAN CATHOLIC CHURCH
The Roman Catholic Archbishop Pius Ncube stood against President Mugabe. In the R. C. Church I discovered a church (where I could find a religious home.)

The Ndlovus as a clan were LMS. But my mother became a Roman Catholic. My sister became sick in 1949, when she was doing Standard 4 at (the Roman Catholic) Empandeni Mission. My mother kept up links with that mission till a Roman Catholic mission was built at Maphisa Growth Point. This was about the time that I was doing Standards One and Two. I became a Catholic when my mother fell sick aged about 91. She was constantly asking me to go to fetch a priest.

My wife and I converted to Catholicism in 2005. I married Lwandle Dube, also part of the Bango clan, in 1970. We had six children: twin daughters, and four boys of whom the last-born died. I have three grandchildren and a great grand- child. But only one of my children, a son, is in Zimbabwe.

MY EMPLOYERS

I was employed by Raisons in 1970. Previously I had temporary jobs in industry- there was lots of industry at that time.

I stayed with Raisons till 1975, when I left and joined a credit controlling company called the Bulawayo Credit Protection Society. In 1980 I joined the ZimBank, then called Rhobank, till 2007, when I was supposed to get my pension. But I got nothing because, that year, the economy collapsed.

I had bought some cattle and I have a truck with which I can ferry people. I do have a very big property and grow vegetables and maize as well as raising chickens. I qualified for NSSA- a pension scheme developed by John Nkomo, from which I get 60 dollars a month.

I was a union member and became a member of the Movement for Democratic Change by virtue of this.

Interviewed by Marieke Clarke at Bulawayo on 7th October 2017

JARET SIBANDA
Entered Inyathi School in 1963

My family was very much involved in the Liberation Struggle. But I never left the country because I struggled here. My brothers, however, were fighting from outside the country. I nearly went too, but I was the only son whom my mother had left at home. She cried so much, when I said I wanted to join the Freedom Struggle, that I stayed in this country to be with her.

My family are some of the core Ndebele people. We were BaSotho people, whom Tshaka integrated into his army as *abenhla* after a war near what is now Lesotho. Perhaps our ancestors were in King Lobhengula's bodyguard with Sihuluhulu Mabhena. The older generation had their ears slit but my generation did not. My mother was from Ntabazinduna and my father was from Entembeni (near Umguza Cement Siding Area).

My maternal grandfather told me that he fought at Gadade and also at Pupu. He never finished telling the story. He would break down and cry and walk away.

My maternal grandfather told me that the royal troops fought so hard at Gadade that the little stream, the Mbembesi, ran with blood. "They were warriors," said my grandfather," but the Pioneer Column was using a cannon[79]. The amaNdebele thought that nothing would come out of the cannon. They would say 'Plug the cannon with your *amabhetshu*.'"

That is, "Vala ngebhetshu!" (Amabhetshu were men's lower garments.)

---
[79] Maxim guns

My maternal grandfather was with his brother in the king's army at Pupu and the brother fell sick, apparently with malaria. The news came that the white men's Pioneer Column was approaching and the royal troops had to move. My grandfather could not leave his brother, so he did the honourable thing and killed his brother.

My family tree goes back to some of the first group of LMS converts after the Conquest. My parents were married in 1928 by W. W. Anderson of the LMS. We were an LMS and Inyathi family. It was a white wedding. [80] I was born in early 1945.

My parents had three sons and one daughter, whom they named Hanna. We all loved that girl as our queen. My father unfortunately became a town-dweller living in a lavish style with female partners and in the process having many children. During those days it was a status symbol to live like that: you became a real man and that was the culture. Because of my father's lifestyle, I had much more to do with my mother's family. (See below).

Our family was forcibly moved from Umguza to Ncema (at Bushtick near Esigodini) where the streams were always full of water. I started my education at the big LMS school there. I did my Sub-standard A to Standard One at Ncema.

We had about ten cattle at Ncema. Every year, the District Commissioner would send a man to tell us: "You must not have more than ten animals." The DC would decide which of the cattle

---

[80] Joshua Mahlathini Mpofu wrote (edited by MFC) "One of the outstanding features of the increase of trained teachers {in the Shangani Reserve} was the advent of fashionable attire at teachers' weddings. The distinguishing features included a Christian ceremony and the bride's white attire from headgear to footwear. Every one of my age glued their hopes on that form of wedding." My life in the struggle for the Liberation of Zimbabwe", page 11.

had to be sold at the DC's price. With those animals the white people- the only ones buying--restocked their herds. Of course they grabbed the best animals.

In 1955 we were moved again, because the whole Ncema area was earmarked for white people to farm. Many black families were moved. We were relocated to Nkayi near Mbuma mission, which was a Free Presbyterian mission.

The Mbuma area was untamed bush. Families were carried by Zeederberg Transport, but we had nobody to walk the cattle. So we formed ourselves into groups of families and it took us eight days on the move to get to Nkayi. We moved with neighbours, not with family members. I personally walked the whole way from Ncema to Nkayi on my bare feet, with no sandals or shoes. The traditional sandals that people used to wear before Conquest had died out with our grandfathers. I had tennis shoes for the first time when I went for admission to Inyathi. Only later did I have "proper" shoes.

We used to start at daybreak and walked till 2 pm. We cooked while the animals grazed. I lost two of our cows from the poisonous herb *umkhawuzane*, which is green even in the dry season: the cows would go for the green and die. This dreadful plant was new to us.

LIFE AT MBUMA
At Ncema we had thought we were modern and we wore shorts (trousers were for white men only) though my grandfather wore *amabhetshu*. At Mbuma some men were still wearing *amabhetshu* too. Some of the people there spoke isiNdebele with a Tonga accent.
Skins were also used for blankets and to sit on.

When I got to Nkayi, I saw a borehole for the first time, as there were no constantly flowing streams. The boreholes were working at that time. But one thing at Shangani was good: you could have as many cattle as you wanted.

AND LEAVING MBUMA

We stayed one year at Mbuma. Then my mother had a visit from her mother's sister, who lived about 30 km away on the Shangani River. My mother decided to move and live with her aunt.

I moved 11 cattle to Sikhobokhobo's place: we settled there with my mother's aunt. We were much better off there. But at Sikhobokhobo's, there was no school providing Standard 2. I crossed the River Shangani and went to a school where I studied up to Standard 3. Then we heard that Standard 4 facilities were being opened at Dakamela's. There I met Jack Nhliziyo and we did Standards 4, 5 and 6 together. He had come from Malinga's.

Jack Nhliziyo was two years ahead of me and went to Inyathi School.[81] When I finished Standard 6, I also got a place at Inyathi, luckily.

INYATHI SCHOOL

I was at Inyathi School between 1963 and 1966. Inyathi was a model school in terms of education and also religion. My brothers paid my school fees so, when they were out of the country, I was left out in the cold. So I stayed at Inyathi School during the holidays. I worked on the school grounds to complement the fees that my mother could not pay, even if she sold a few chickens and goats.

We were privileged to attend Inyathi School, which had a very rich history since 1859.

---

[81] See chapter on Jack Nhliziyo.

Now and then, in our youth, things were hard. You could not socialise as you can today. There was too much red tape in our lives, which were tailored by the white regime. You were supposed to be happy with this. Do you realise, Marieke, that the whole school cried when you were deported?

When we fought for our freedom, which was a normal thing to do, we were actually fighting for our identity, our right to live and also our right to choose.

Things were very hard for us in terms of education and jobs, because of UDI.[82] I think most of us would have gone higher and higher. There were a limited number of reserved school places for blacks. It did not matter how intelligent you were, there were limited opportunities further than that.[83] You hit a ceiling and had to change course.

The unique thing about Inyathi School was that most of the teachers were expatriates and distinguished in their own countries. The quality of education was second to none, though the laboratory was poor.

The students' spoken English was excellent, because they had to speak English 6 days a week: we students could only speak isiNdebele on Sundays.

After Form 4, I could go no further because there was no money for my school fees. I came to Bulawayo in 1967 and could choose

---

[82] The Rhodesian white minority regime declared independence of Britain in November 1965.
[83] It was a policy of the white minority regime to limit the number of secondary school places for black students. This was so that whites could occupy most of the important jobs.

between two or three jobs. I resigned from a job at 1 pm and started another at 2 pm.

In 1968 I went to Salisbury for a job interview with about ten other people. The interviewers looked at my testimonials and I was asked only one question: "Are you from Inyathi School?" and got the job. The interview ended with me.

But what was hard was integrating. I was the first African clerk in the history of the company I worked for: it was a breakthrough. Three white women refused to work with me and left. The owner of the company was a good man, a Jew called Ernest Hoder. The company made furniture.

SUPPORTING THE FREEDOM MOVEMENT
WHILE WORKING IN BULAWAYO

While I was working in town, every weekend I would go home to Shangani with a list of items that the guerrillas wanted, for instance boots and jeans. Shangani was the base of most ZPRA cadres: by 1975 there were more guerrillas than Smith had soldiers.

My car had seat covers under which I would hide the jeans and the boots, for fear of roadblocks. The people of Shangani were very supportive of the guerrillas, but the locals were being clobbered left, right and centre.

If guerrillas passed through a neighbourhood, the white soldiers would be in hot pursuit and blame local people for looking after the guerrillas. Similarly, if the Smith soldiers came first, the guerrillas followed them and blamed the locals. Many people were beaten for no reason. We had an exodus of young people, especially, moving into town doing surveillance for the Liberation Movement.

THOUGHTS ABOUT THE LONDON MISSIONARY SOCIETY

The LMS had the best choice of the missionary societies because most Ndebele people, that is ZAPU people, are descendants of the LMS. Women were very much empowered by the LMS, because the majority of church people were women. The Ndebele men, on the other hand, believed that a man had three kingdoms: i) meat; ii) beer; iii) women..
Men thought they must be the master of these three.

The missionaries visited homes and encouraged women to be self-sufficient and to bring their children to school. If it had not been for the LMS, my mother would not have been as strong as she was. She got moral support and empowerment from the missionaries.

It was hard for men to send their children to school. If boys were sent to school, who would herd the cattle? And the men thought that girls were only useful as a source of lobola money as bearers of children.
Missionaries had to break through the barrier of the women to allow daughters to go to school. Men tended to think that educating girls was putting money into someone else's home.

AFTER I STARTED TO WORK

After I started to work, I went to night school, did management courses, studied Human Resources and Business Studies. I rose up the ranks to be Department Superintendent, Production Manager/Factory Manager/Sales and Marketing and finally in 1969 General Manager in Mr Hoder's company. I worked for that company for 47 years and left 8 years ago. The company then called me back on contract. The company has been going for 95 years.

MY RETIREMENT

I have land at Esigodini near Ncema that I bought in 1978. I do charity work. I have seven children of whom two are in the UK, two in South Africa and three here in Zimbabwe.

OUR FAMILY TRAGEDY

Our great family tragedy concerns our sister Hanna (Mrs Nkomo), who was trained as a teacher at Hope Fountain. In 1983 she was teaching at Singwangombe. Gukurahundi had reached the area. She had just come out of the school and reached home. Armed soldiers seized her, threw her into a hut and set it on fire: she died. Two weeks later we family members went to the place. We buried the ashes of the hut and of our beloved sister and also of her niece "Thabani". The little girl could not bear to watch this gruesome murder and screamed loudly! To silence her, the armed soldiers grabbed her and threw her into the burning hut, and she died with her aunt: Hanna had been the queen of our family.

Interviewed by Marieke Clarke at Bulawayo on 5th October 2017

MUSA "DADE" DUNGENI (nee MHLOPHE)
She entered Inyathi School in 1964.

I was born to Mr. and Mrs. Magwamazi Elijah Mhlophe of Glass Block (Ematshetsheni) in Gwanda District under Chief Mzimuni Masuku on 10 August 1950.

My parents named me Ntombiyomusa, but Native Commissioner Hubbard, who found it difficult to pronounce my long name, registered me as Musa. My mother, Tanana Khumalo, was of royal blood; her father Mpinda was the son of Mbehane, the son of King Mzilikazi Khumalo. My paternal great grandfather was Mpeme while my grandfather was Mpehlane, father to Magwamazi Elijah Mhlophe.

At Glass Block we belonged to the London Missionary Society (LMS), which later became known as the United Congregational Church of Southern Africa (UCCSA), where my father was church leader for the local congregation. The LMS was brought to our area from Hope Fountain Mission. Reverend Sitshenkwa Hlabangana at one time lived in the Essexvale area (now known as Esigodini) and ministered to the Amatshetshe, who were at that time located close by, before they were moved to where they currently live.

In 1956 I enrolled for Sub Standard A and attended Glass Block Primary School, where Mr. Ezra Gwebu was Head Teacher. Some of the staff at the school were Cephas Cele, Jacob Nyoni who operated Siye Phambili Store, and Richard Tshili, who, on account of my brightness in class, approached my father and said to him, "If your daughter fails Standard 6, I will give you a beast."

It was, however, Mr Cele who was a political animal. One day a man arrived at our school on a scooter. Mr. Cele asked the pupils in his class to leave the classroom to have a look at the two-wheeled contraption. On its body was emblazoned, in capital letters, 'NYIKA NDEYEDU." I was later to learn that the words meant, 'The country is ours.' Apparently, Mr. Cele was to join ZAPU's Special Affairs Department and trained as a guerrilla at Morogoro in Tanzania. He served in ZPRA's High Command. When he died, he was buried at the National Heroes Acre in Harare.

I was well gifted in class and teachers sometimes asked me to sit examinations with higher classes, whom I beat hands down. They would then be beaten for poor performance. In 1963 I completed Standard 6 and went to do Form 1 at Inyathi Mission. The LMS was the link. When I got to Inyathi Mission in 1964, Kenneth Maltus Smith was the Principal. He was a militarily inclined person who had participated in World War II.[84] When the school bell rang, he used to stand at attention and when we saw him, we ran fast. The man was a disciplinarian. The other teachers were Mr Henry Undy, Mr Themba Nhlapo, Mr Philip Symes, Mr D. Flood, Miss Mary Austin and Mr Kono Ndlovu whom we nicknamed Dederos.

The following were some of the students that I still remember: Sithabile Ndlovu (sister to Dederos), Gertrude Ngwenya the Head Girl, now Mrs. Gertrude Nyakutse, Victor George Ndlovu, Jack Nhliziyo, Ezlyn Sibanda, Gilfiny Masuku the feared school boy,

---

[84] Marieke Clarke, who taught under Kenneth Maltus Smith, believes this was impossible as Ken would have been too young. But Marieke believes that Ken did National Service, which was compulsory for British young men after World War Two till 1959.

Sibonile Mhlophe, Ottilia Sebata the Deputy Head Girl, Tivington Ncube, Vivian Mguni, (now Mrs. Ncube), Robert Moyo, Roger Mthethwa, Bekithemba Lusinga, Berita Khumalo and Samukeliso Ndebele. We belonged to school "houses" named after early missionaries at Inyathi: Sykes(William Sykes), Thomas(Thomas Morgan Thomas), Rees(Bowen Rees) and Moffat(Reverend Dr Robert Moffat). I belonged to Moffat House. We used to compete against other LMS schools: Dombodema Mission and Hope Fountain Mission, now Tennyson Hlabangana.

There were many factors that accounted for our politicization at Inyathi. One reason was that, in our midst there were mature students such as Jack Nhliziyo from Nkayi. Some of these students had experienced brutal evictions from places such as Fort Rixon (Emakhandeni) and Filabusi.

Another reason was that we learned about Current Affairs even at primary school level and this subject continued at Inyathi. We were kept abreast of political events taking place around the world, from what was taking place at home to events happening in the United States of America and the United Kingdom.

It was however, dramatization of plays which was the most captivating and inspiring factor in our politicisation. We did not dramatize plays in some hall or other school building. Rather, drama was enacted in the open air. There were themes and values such as justice and equality that were brought out and had lasting effects on our minds. The "Merchant of Venice" was one such Shakespearean play that was performed. I still have a vivid memory of Jack Nhliziyo playing the role of King Duncan in "Macbeth"[85].

---

[85] This production took place in the reedy area from which the old name of Inyathi- Emhlangeni- was taken.MFC

Our school library had supplementary books that we read. Books like "Mntanami Mntanami" by Sibusiso Nyembezi, and many others in English cultivated, in us, some sense of political consciousness. One book that I still remember well was "The Man," a book that broadened my horizons. One character was an Afro-American whom the whites would not vote for on grounds of his race. The book exposed me to ills of racism, a socio-political phenomenon that was the hallmark of Southern Rhodesia.

I was to experience the scourge of racism at a time when we had expatriate teachers who became our friends, one of whom was Musgrave. We used to frequent the Hillside Dams in Bulawayo: whites who were picnicking there would move away when they saw us approach them. It was the same in restaurants. We were shunned like a people afflicted with leprosy. Sadly, our own people in the Western Suburbs of Bulawayo viewed us as political sellouts when they saw us in the company of the same expatriate teachers.

Inyathi Mission was an iconic site for student activism. I remember well the incident when students boycotted meals in the Dining Hall. The militarily inclined Principal, Mr Smith, paced into the hall and stood menacingly in front of Wise Dube, who was known to be an activist. Looking Wise in the eyes, Mr Smith boomed, "Pick up your spoon. Dip it into the porridge. Take it out with porridge. Put it into your mouth. Take it out of your mouth without porridge. Swallow!" After Wise Dube, Mr Smith sauntered towards the next student, also viewed as an activist. Mr Symes adopted a similar strategy when students refused to take porridge.

"Why are you not eating this porridge?"

"It's undercooked, Sir." Mr Symes would then proceed to eat the porridge to prove it could be consumed.

There were times when church services were boycotted. Students marched to where services were conducted. Boys, as a mark of protest, went ahead and blocked entrances to the church building. Protests and strikes were the enduring culture at Inyathi Mission.

At the end of 1965 I sat for the Rhodesia Junior Certificate (RJC) examinations and passed with credits in English and Arithmetic. All in all, I had the required six subjects. At the time Mr Ken Smith had left Inyathi Mission for Moeding College in Bechuanaland (now Botswana) and Mr Undy became the Principal. We went home on school holidays, during which we received our results.

Undy disappointed me greatly. He wrote this remark, "Well done, however cannot come for Form 3. Rather immature." We were two classes in Form 2 but there was to be only one Form 3 class. True, I was young in age and small in body stature, but to say immature was rather too extreme. For a whole year I was at home.

In 1967 I enrolled at the Salvation Army's Usher Institute near Figtree, where I trained as a Domestic Science teacher. Major Gardner was the Principal. One teacher whom I remember was Botshiwe Ngwenya who did not seem to like me. My physical stature was still small and, when I completed the course, members of staff would not let me go loose to be preyed upon by predators in schools. As a result, schools were consulted regarding existing teaching vacancies.

I landed a teaching post at Hope Fountain Mission where Japhet Mabaleka was Head Teacher. He was to become my English teacher at a time when he headed Mzingwane Government School for boys. I was then teaching at Essexvale and doing evening classes. For our lessons we went to Esikhoveni Public Service Training Centre. I posted passes in English language, English Literature, Commerce, IsiNdebele and Geography. I taught at several schools including Tegwane School of the Wesleyan Methodist Church at a time when the Liberation War had ratcheted up a few notches. School pupils were abducted by ZPRA guerrillas and driven to Botswana. However, following the Headmaster, Luke Mawogelana Khumalo's, appeal, some pupils were allowed to return.

For some time I became a rolling stone of sorts. I taught at schools such as Rumhuma, Amaveni before landing a post at Hyde Park School in rural Mpopoma, outside Pumula Location. At the time, Independence had not been attained. I was active in nationalist politics, being involved in the activities of ZAPU's Women's League.

At one time we were bundled into a police truck and taken to Stops Police Camp in Bulawayo. ZAPU was still a banned political movement in Zimbabwe-Rhodesia at that time. When asked where I worked, I responded that I was unemployed. That response earned me my freedom. Other ladies answered in similar manner and we all escaped incarceration.

Even at home in Glass Block, politics were spoken about in hushed tones. Chief Mzimuni Masuku was a staunch supporter of the Smith regime. Whenever NDP and ZAPU activists were arrested, he used to speak in glowing terms about their predicament. "They have been castrated," he would gloat. At one time a petrol bomb was thrown into his big house, resulting in a massive crater. My father spoke in muted tones about political events in the Matshetsheni area.

The highlight came in 1980 when I was teaching in Essexvale. ZPRA, ZAPU's armed wing, was bringing in its armoured tanks from Zambia, via Gwayi Assembly Point. They came in low-loaders and were taken into the custody of ZPRA cadres. The little town came to a standstill. Stores were closed as people came to see the war arsenal that they had never seen before. *"Buya bona kaloyinto kaloNkomo!"* ("Come and see Joshua Nkomo's war arsenal.")

I continued with my studies when I taught at Montrose High School in Bulawayo where Mrs. Cross was Headmistress. After graduating with a B. Ed degree, I proceeded to do a Master's degree. I was then on my way to becoming Head of School. After some time at How Mine, I eventually became Head of Khumalo Primary School till my retirement in 2015. The previous year, my school had won the Secretary's Merit Award, a fitting conclusion to my long career as a teacher.

When others pursued political activism, I became active in the Zimbabwe Teachers' Association, ZIMTA. I became the editor of ZIMTA's newspaper, the Teachers' Voice in Zimbabwe (TVZ). We were fighting injustice, the sort of injustice that we had been alerted to at Inyathi Mission. I was active in the education of teachers and also in the study circles where we dealt with HIV/Aids issues. As African teachers, we were left to deal with HIV-related issues. We partnered with the American Federation of Teachers and visited Washington where we undertook work place programmes for teachers.

In 1976 Morris Dungeni and I tied the knot and went to live at Enqostheni, also referred to as Geneva [86]. In 1976 constitutional talks were held in Geneva, Switzerland, in an effort to end the Rhodesian constitutional impasse. We later relocated to Waterford[87]. We were blessed with three children; Gugulethu, Bhekizulu and Dalubuhle.
Interview by Pathisa Nyathi

---

[86] A Bulawayo township built in 1976, when the Geneva Talks were held.
[87] An eastern suburb of Bulawayo where Musa and her husband live.

SIBONGILE MAPHINI (nee MOYO)
She entered Inyathi School in 1965

I was born on 18th October 1949 at Tshankwa in the then Bulilima-Mangwe District to Moses, whose wife was Ruth Bulu. Ntuswa was my paternal grandfather and MaSongo was his wife. There were nine of us in the family, six girls and three boys. My father originally came from Gwambe near Tegwane Mission, which was run by Wesleyan Methodists.

My father worked at Plumtree High School for white boys. While there, he was advised by missionaries and school authorities to do teacher training at Tegwane Mission. My early life was spent more in hospital at Plumtree General Hospital than at home. Initially, my condition was not diagnosed. My primary education was interrupted by my condition and I had to repeat Standard 6 in the hope that the condition was going to improve. There was a time when it was suspected I suffered from Tuberculosis (TB).

It was only when I was tested at Mpilo Hospital in Bulawayo that it was discovered I was allergic to cats and to dust. It was then that we came to know that what we had thought was an asthmatic condition was actually an allergy. I enrolled for Sub-Standard A at Tshankwa Primary School in 1956. I had to repeat Standard 6 in 1963 because of ill health. I thus completed primary education in 1964. My health condition was mentioned in my end of year report by the medical doctor and the missionaries.

Some of the teachers at Tshankwa were my mother, Mrs Moyo, and my father, who was the Head Teacher. Other teachers at the school were Ms Dube, Mr Ndebele, Mr Obed Mnyama, Mr Zitha and Mr Khabo.

As a result of my poor health, I was denied a Form 1 vacancy at Tegwane Mission. When it was thought that my condition was going to improve, it actually worsened. But in 1965, I moved from hospital to Inyathi Mission where Mr Ken Maltus Smith was Principal. Other members of staff were Mary Austin, Themba Nhlapo, Mr Symes, 'Makhakhi' Ndlovu and Mzingaye Dube.

When I moved to Inyathi Mission, my health improved drastically. I had been given six injections and it became clear there was something I was allergic to among the things found in certain parts of Plumtree. Consequently, I now spent most of my time in Bulawayo. My condition seemed to prefer cold and drizzly conditions. I felt really good when staying in the cool Eastern Highlands. Excited about my condition, I wrote to my mother, "Mama, now I am able to run. My afflictions are over."

At Inyathi Mission I intermingled with pupils from various places and primary schools that were feeder schools for Inyathi Mission. Some of these pupils were Jean Dlamini, Ottilia Sebata, Themba Mpofu, Mthandazo Ndema Ngwenya, Christopher Sibanda, Njabulo Khabo[88], Jareth Ndlovu, and Robert Moyo the Head Boy. I remember very vividly when I arrived at Inyathi Mission kneeling before one of the school boys. I thought he was one of the teachers, because he was a grown up man. I only discovered that he was a school pupil when I saw him in uniform on Monday.

During the second term of 1966 there were disturbances at Inyathi School. We went on strike following decisions by school authorities to reduce or completely cut off food rations and other commodities that we had hitherto been receiving. Ten o'clock tea was discontinued. Rations for both powdered and bar soap were

---

[88] Son of Jeremiah Khabo (See separate chapter)

reduced. There was resistance from some students, all the more so considering that our parents had not been informed about the decisions.

The entire school was suspended for two weeks. Some pupils, including Mthandazo Ndema Ngwenya and Christopher Sibanda, were expelled. However, some parents made appeals to school authorities and the pupils were reinstated. The issue became a hot potato when the Member of Parliament, Mafavuke Mhlanga, got involved. He summoned some pupils to interviews so he could get to the bottom of the matter. Mr Mhlanga used to drive to Bulawayo to attend court sessions involving some pupils.

Inyathi Mission, like other mission boarding schools, subjected new pupils to rough initiation treatment. The newcomers, mostly Form 1 pupils, were referred to as *amanyunyu (the new ones)* or *madzvinyu* (lizards). All manner of rough treatment was visited upon them. Douglas Dube was one pupil who was rough to newcomers. One time he tied a newcomer to a dormitory roof. When other students drew his attention to the fact that the student was on the verge of dying, he nonchalantly said, *Yekela kufe okuliShona,*"Let the Shona die." Ethnic sentiments already existed.

When the tradition of roughing up new students was reported to the Principal, Mr Smith, he said, "Have you not seen what a new beast goes through when it enters a cattle pen? Doesn't it get attacked by other beasts? So, what is the issue here?" One pupil, Leonard, had been stabbed with a knife. New girls, out of fear, attached themselves to some senior boys as a way of seeking protection from molesters. My protector was John Maphini, then not my boyfriend. I only fell in love with him when I was at Hope Fountain Mission where I was training as an infant teacher.

Inyathi Mission had two streams in Forms 1 and 2. However, there was a bottleneck when we got to Form 3 where there was only one class. Those pupils who did not make the grade in academic or behavioural terms were left out. A few pupils from other schools were taken on board. So it was with me. I did not make it to Form 3 at Inyathi Mission. As a result, I went to enrol for teacher training at Hope Fountain Mission, another LMS institution.

What a difference there was between the two LMS institutions! Hope Fountain Mission was not bedevilled by school protests, boycotts and strikes. It was all peaceful.

The only incident that caused concern in either 1967 or 1968 was a serious earth tremor. So severe it was that plates and cups on tables shook and fell off. We got the feeling of being suspended and great fear gripped us.

The diet at Hope Fountain was markedly different from that at Inyathi Mission. The Principal was Macdonald Partridge, who was affectionately known as Nkwali, the Ndebele name for a bird called partridge. It was he who would later open the multidenominational teacher training college called the United College of Education (UCE) which was handed over to government when my husband John Maphini was Acting Principal. Lessons for pioneering students were conducted at Msiteli Secondary School, an F2 school in Mpopoma Township in Bulawayo. Lecturers at the college included Mr Ndondo, Mr Masosomere, Mildred Ndlovu, (later Mrs Mkandla)[89], and Mr Gobert. The secondary component, which ended at Form 2 level, was headed by Mr S. P. Ndlovu. Some fellow trainees that I remember were Thembekile Gumede, (later Mrs Mhlophe), Miriam Mabaleka, Sithembile Nyoni, (later Mrs

---

[89] See chapter on her.

Mahlangu), Menradis the daughter of Mrs S P Ndlovu, (later Mrs Shoniwa). We were specializing in infant teaching with our course being referred to as T4.

When I completed teacher training in 1968, I went to teach at St Patrick's Mission in Chiwundura where Reverend Elliot V. S. Dhlula was Principal. My husband went to teach at Howard Institute, which belonged to the Salvation Army. It was at a time when the Zimbabwe African National Liberation Army (ZANLA) forces, the armed wing of the Zimbabwe African National Union (ZANU) had penetrated the northeast corner of Rhodesia, now Zimbabwe. The people in Chiweshe and other adjoining areas had been hounded by the Smith regime into what were referred to as Keeps, an arrangement meant to sever links between guerrillas and villagers who were supporting their cause and thus supplying them with intelligence and other necessities such as food and clothing.

I was not teaching then, but I was asked to attend to the needs of villagers, who were brought to Nyachuru and dumped at 4.00 pm in open ground in winter when the nights were bitterly cold. We fed the desperate mothers who were nursing their children.

When my husband went to the University of Zimbabwe (UZ) for further education, our children and I relocated to Bulawayo. We had been at Howard Institute from 1973 to 1974. We left for Bulawayo in 1975. I taught at Masuku Primary School from 1977 to March 1982. I then went to teach at Matshayisikhova Primary School in Luveve from March to October 1982, when I transferred to Kumalo Primary School where I remained till my retirement in 2014.

Between 1985 and 1987, I was doing private studies leading to an "O" Level Certificate. I studied through the Central African Correspondence College (CACC). I used to write examinations in

June and again in January, as I worked full time as a teacher. At each sitting, I wrote two subjects. I proceeded to do a B.Ed degree with the University of Zimbabwe (UZ) through distance education from 1996 to 1998.

I got married to John Maphini in 1971 at Tshankwa. My father asked me if I had told my partner about my health condition. Indeed, John was quite aware, but only after my father was satisfied did he demand *amalobolo* from John Maphini. We had two children, Pilile, born in 1970 before we got married, and now late, and Andrew, our son, born in 1971. My husband passed on in 2017.

Interview by Pathisa Nyathi

RODGER MUHLWA
Entered Inyathi School 1967

My paternal grandfather had been one of King Lobhengula's aides and scattered when the kingdom fell. My grandfather ended up at Shurugwi. He was a herbalist, a traditional doctor, who assisted the king. My grandfather learned the medical skills from his forefathers. He told us he did so via dreams.

While the kingdom was collapsing, my grandfather was instructed in dreams to go and settle in Gokwe, and so he was cut off from his people. After some years, my grandfather heard from the runners[90] that Ndebele people were being settled in the Shangani Reserve bordering on Gokwe where he lived among the Sankwe (Shangwe) people. So he decided to relocate from Gokwe to live among his own kith and kin at Nkayi.

My grandfather, originally a Mthethwa but who had since become a Muhlwa, settled at Ezidulini, the place of anthills, under Chief Dakamela Ncube. The sparsely populated space provided good grazing. My grandfather chose to settle at Ezidulini because the place offered adequate grazing for his large herd. Chief Dakamela was a friend of my grandfather and the area was settled with Ndebele-speaking people.

MY FATHER'S MARRIAGES

I was born at Ezidulini. My father was fairly well to do. He had more than 100 head of cattle. My father had two wives, MaLunga of

---

[90] Under the Ndebele kingdom there had been a system of runners who conveyed information extremely fast. This system continued for some time after the collapse of the kingdom.

Sankwe origin, and my own mother, MaDube, the younger wife. My father married MaDube after MaLunga had her eighth and final child. He had six children with my mother (therefore 14 children altogether).

MY MOTHER

My mother was born in 1922. I was her first son and therefore responsible for the rest of her children.

When my father died, MaLunga and her sons abandoned MaDube, saying she had been the favourite wife. To make a living, my mother would weave baskets and mats. After harvest she would come to town walking door to door bartering the baskets in exchange for second hand clothes. She also earned money from selling pigs, a practice considered taboo for Seventh Day Adventist people.

My mother wove baskets because, after my father's death, there were not enough cattle to sell. Besides, my mother thought it prudent to save the cattle for us when we were grown up.

After my father died, my mother could have married my paternal uncle through the system of *ukungena*, but my mother refused to do so. Instead, taking us six children and our cattle, she went back to her birth family at Siyali, not very far away from where we had been living before my father died. You can cycle that distance in a day.

MY EDUCATION

From the point of view of the modern world, I came from a poor background. Both my parents were illiterate. I had to plough before I went to school and without having breakfast. Two of the sons of MaLunga (older than me) got good education.

My father died when I was doing Sub Standard A. My mother did her best to send me to school. I grew up with my mother's brothers. My mother was head of her own household. Her brothers were not in control of us, but they did give advice.

I attended schools at Ezidulini and Gampinya. These provided education up to Standard 1, so I went to stay with my half-sister at Dakamela. She had no son and regarded me as her son. I went to Upper Primary when I was living with her.

Where we lived was a backward area and few people appreciated the importance of education. When I was doing Standard Three, I was regarded as very educated. Life was very tough for my mother. Because of lack of manpower, she could not grow many crops.

When I finished Standard Six, I got a place at Dombodema to do my secondary education. I was offered a place at several schools including Inyathi, but I preferred to go to Dombodema as it offered new experiences. I was going to see Bulawayo, get on a bus and travel by train from Bulawayo to Plumtree by train. But Dombodema Secondary School only had Forms One and Two.

The fees at Dombodema cost £36 for the whole year and the cost of the first term was £15. I went to my half-brother, a teacher, asking him to pay my fees on loan. He replied that I did not need to repay the fees, but said instead, "Come and live with me and help around the place."
The first term he did pay the fees.

At Dombodema I repaired furniture at the school, in return for pay, and so raised my pocket money. At my previous school I had learned some carpentry. When schools closed for term 1, my teacher half- brother left me stranded at Dombodema School, so I had no bus

fare to get home. I played dice and made enough money to get to Bulawayo and bought a Terylene skirt for my mother. They were very popular at the time and I knew my mother would like it.
When I got back to my teacher half-brother's place to help him, I overslept the following morning. Nobody woke me or offered me breakfast. I went to the fields, where my half-brother told me that he could not pay my school fees. I cried. I walked to my mother's place without having breakfast. We cried and we prayed.

I approached a store holder at Dakamela –he was called Mr Dearth-- together with my former head teacher at Dakamela, who knew me well. I told Mr Dearth my story and Mr Dearth agreed to pay my fees at Dombodema. He said, "You don't need to work for me, but do send me a report from school."

I got a Beit scholarship to go to Form Three and so went to Inyathi.
With this very insecure background, I could not participate in any risky activities at school. But I idolised Joshua Nkomo. Both my mother and I bought ZAPU cards, thinking, "We shall keep this card till Joshua Nkomo comes to power. Otherwise we might be in trouble."

We found a mopane tree with a hole in it. I put the cards in plastic in the hole so that the police could never find it.

When I came home from Dakamela, I found that all the trees around the mopane tree in which I had hidden the letter had been cleared. I walked and searched and searched and finally saw a paper-like thing: the card- flying. I certainly wanted things in this country to change. I admired some of the ZAPU people very much.

I was at Inyathi School in 1967-8 to do Forms Three and Four. Inyathi had debates like a mini-United Nations. After UDI in 1965, repression descended ruthlessly on anyone with views that were opposed: therefore things at Inyathi were much quieter than they had been earlier.

To have known Ken Maltus Smith as our headmaster was great. He was very straight. I became deputy head boy. Millius Palayiwa Ncube was head boy at the time.

PLANNING FOR WORK

When I was at Inyathi School, students in Form Four filled in an application form about their future plans. I said I wanted to get a job. Ken Smith understood precisely. He asked if I had found work. I said "No". He asked me to be the school clerk. By March of 1969, I had learned to type and was doing all the school typing including exam papers. I also gained a driver's licence and became the school driver. I was paid £25 a month.[91]

Ken left to go to Moeding College in Botswana in 1968. Philip Symes (with whom I am still in touch) took over as headmaster.[92]

Road Motor Services collected orders for the school. The RMS driver told me that the railways were recruiting.[93] I passed the tests and got a job on the railway. I earned good overtime payment as a fireman. Politics then got to me.

Three men would work on the footplate of a train fuelled by coal. I was a fireman who shovelled coal into the engine furnace. The train

---

[91] Marieke Clarke in 1963/4 was paid about £100 a month to work as a teacher at the school but she paid no rent, water or electricity costs for her two-bedroomed home..

[92] Philip Symes taught Science in 1963/4. He was principal for three years.

[93] White men were leaving the country fast to avoid being called up into the armed forces, so the government needed black people to do jobs that had previously been reserved exclusively for whites.

driver was an uneducated white man. They were recruited as white men from all over the world. An uneducated African worker would push the coal closer for the fireman. The driver would not exchange a word with me, but he would talk in a racist way to the unskilled worker beside me. This behaviour helped me to become more politicised. I used to say "A minority has never won against a majority."

On the railways I could progress. The station master chose me for administrative work when the war was hot. I lost overtime by changing jobs but became operating clerk. I was one of the first five blacks to do administrative work on the railways as the whites fled the country.

I was invited to become the first black station foreman in the country and then the first black stationmaster in Zimbabwe. I worked on the railways for 23 years and rose to the top to be Operations Manager. Because of tribalism on the railways, I took early retirement.

I retired early and cashed in my pension. Now I do market gardening for a living, working near Bulawayo.

**MY CONTRIBUTION TO THE FREEDOM STRUGGLE
WHILE I WAS WORKING ON THE RAILWAYS**

In the 1970's many young people wanted to go to Zambia. They would phone me and I would take them in my private car as far as Tsholotsho. Once I took Cephas Msipa's[94] son across in the staff coach on the train. When I was working on the trains that ran up and down the line from Botswana to what we hoped would soon be Zimbabwe, I had freedom fighters sheltering in the staff carriage on the train so the police could not find them.

---

[94] Cephas Msipa: 1931-2016, Educationalist and politician. Governor of Midlands Province.

CONCLUSION

I had a clever mother who had over 50 cattle. Children whom I knew had neither clever parents nor cattle. Their lives were written off from the start. Without education in Rhodesia, a black person had nothing. There were not enough secondary schools for black students in Rhodesia and there are still not enough secondary schools in Matabeleland. Inyathi is still the only school between Bulawayo and Nkayi that has sixth form classes. Yet in Mashonaland there is a school every three kilometres. At Nkayi there is Hlangabeza that was started on the initiative of the Governor Welshman Mabhena.

I married Rita whom I had known at Dombodema and Inyathi Schools. She did a secretarial course and worked in Edgars Stores in the marketing department and then as credit co-ordinator.

Pathisa Nyathi comments: Rodger Muhlwa was known as "The mayor" when as yet Bulawayo had no black mayor. Rodger became chairman of the famous Bulawayo Football Club, the Highlanders.

Rodger Muhlwa last met Ken Maltus Smith in the UK in 2014, the year before he died. "I had last met him in Botswana in 1980. But he remembered me clearly even over the phone. He looked out my exam results in the files he kept of every student at Inyathi School."

Rodger was interviewed by Marieke Clarke on 3rd October 2017 and by Pathisa Nyathi in June 2018

BRIAN MZANA MTHIMKHULU
Entered Inyathi School in 1968

MY CHILDHOOD

Though both my parents were Ndebele, I was brought up in Kwaduma (usually called Gatooma or Kadoma). My mother had been Seventh Day Adventist in her youth but changed to the LMS when she married my father. There was no LMS presence in Kwaduma, so we attended the Methodist Church services. The first qualification that my father, Gerald Mthimkhulu, gained was in agriculture and then he went to Inyathi. The missionary principal Mr Alfred E. Walden[95] turned Gerald into a teacher. The family of the former principal Walden became my father's second home.

My father worked with Welshman Mabhena when they were teachers at Inyathi. My father became a headmaster in 1958 when I was four years old. He was not in the Liberation Struggle. My father insisted that I should go to Inyathi School because he had faith in the LMS.

ACTIVITIES AT INYATHI SCHOOL

We had a strike about food in my first year. In my fourth year, in 1971, a number of students made anti-government posters and stuck these up around the school in the hall and the classrooms. The missionary and Science Teacher Philip Symes had succeeded Ken Smith as head, but only stayed three years.

The posters were in two languages: in isiNdebele they read: "Ilizwe ngelethu, amabhunu zhii" which means "The country is ours. We will destroy the Boers" (ie the white people).

---

[95] Principal of Inyathi School 1939-1955

Police came from the Inyathi Government camp over a weekend and took down the posters. When the police asked who had made the posters, Stephen Mpofu challenged them. He was my classmate and one of the most radical students.

He asked the local police: "What business have you to come to our school?" He was taken away to the police station. We marched towards the police station to liberate Stephen. The police threatened to shoot us. They beat us up severely, both boys and girls. Judith Todd wrote an article about the episode in the magazine *Moto* when she heard about it.

Then the Bulawayo police came and made the whole school, all 230 students, write: "What you want". These police came back two weeks later and said again to the whole school: "Write again".

A week later, the police came back a third time and chose about 15 students to come and write all day. What surprised us students was that most of the 15 who were in the last group, and who had to write all day, had in fact written the posters. These students had tried to disguise their handwriting during the first session, but could not keep up the disguise two weeks later.

I was one of the 15 students. Pheneal Rugare Maphosa was another. Stella Simela was the only girl.

Why did the police require this? I think the reason was that they thought, "When you get really tired, you'll write what you really want." Also they probably wanted to force us to use our real handwriting so as to identify the poster writers.

I think that the school authorities stopped the police investigation, saying that the mid- year exams were about to take place.

MY LIFE AFTER INYATHI SCHOOL.

After Form Four, I worked for three years as a school clerk at Bulawayo and then went to London, where I stayed with my cousin Walter Mthimkhulu, who had been a member of the March 11th movement. (See chapter on Walter). Walter had been at Inyathi in the late 1950's and after Form Four went to Fletcher High School and from there into ZAPU. That showed me that someone could go into the struggle.

Other members of his group were Strike Mkandla[96], Eli Mthethwa, Cain Mathema and Joshua Mahlathini Mpofu (See chapter about him).

When Joshua Nkomo and other leaders came to the UK in 1975, Walter and his group thought that they were going to have the chance to explain why they had revolted against the leadership. But Joshua Nkomo was now surrounded by the very same people whom Walter and his group had arrested. The people who had been arrested set Joshua Nkomo against Walter Mthimkhulu and his group. The group was initially called the Walter group because, as a journalist, my cousin was the best known of the group. I prefer to use the label March 11 Movement, used by Owen Tshabangu, one of the 40 members of the March 11th Movement who went to the UK in 1974.

I did A. levels in Scotland, and then went to the North London Polytechnic[97] where I did a Social Science degree. My dissertation was on the March 11th Movement.

---

[96] Who married our interviewee Mildred Ndlovu.
[97] Now the London Metropolitan University

I returned to Zimbabwe in 1980. I was in the Ministry of Labour for two years and then in Zim Bank for two years. And then I worked for Anglo-American. Then I ran a family grocery store in Bulawayo for Walter's father. Up to 2014, I was manager of Human Resources for Dunlop, Zimbabwe. *Interview by Marieke Clarke on 9th October 2016*

REMEMBERING KENNETH MALTUS SMITH

On 4th October 2015, I attended the memorial service of a man I hold in high esteem. Kenneth Maltus Smith was a teacher and headmaster at Inyathi Mission from 1957 to 1968. He was my headmaster in 1968 when I was in Form 1.

Reverend Kenneth Maltus Smith was born on 22 November 1926 in Jammalamadugu, India and died on 19 September 2015 in Norwich, United Kingdom. He was buried on 5 October 2015.

Ndodana, (Son), as we Inyathi students called him, in reference to the way he pronounced the word without a trace of his English tongue, loved to lunch with students at the Ukuthula Akubekini Dining Hall. I still picture him sitting on the bench at the corner of the prefects' table up on stage wolfing down *isitshwala* and beans. The man always left his plate cleaner than the bald top of his head. Rumour had it that, to try and win back her husband for lunch, Mrs Smith had tried to cook *isitshwala*, but the poor lady could not match the high standards of Mr Mbambo, the mission chef.

"I don't understand you gentlemen,"' Ndodana teased us one Saturday morning. "You complain that you are not getting enough food, but after every meal I see several big dishes of leftovers." Standing up erect on the dining hall stage, he smiled, indicating that it was one of the occasions he lifted his authoritarian mask and wanted to reason with us.

"You see, sir," Johnson, a student in Form 3 said, "In our culture a man does not completely sweep his plate. Oh no! That would be saying 'I am a greedy pig.' A real man must leave something in the plate. We love practising our culture and what better way of showing it by never sweeping our plates?"

I did not know the meaning of the word 'culture' but I joined in when other boys shouted "We love our culture."

"I know the culture," Ndodana said, "but, remember, leftovers at your homes are never thrown away. It is food for dogs and chickens. Neither dogs nor chickens are part of this school. Who are you leaving the food for?"

"It is our culture!" we shouted.

"Think about it," Ndodana chuckled and walked away.

"Guys, I think Ndodana is right", Park Ncube, a dormitory mate later said after lights were switched off. A friend of his agreed. "At a boarding school there is no need to leave food. We should...."

"Huh," Albert sneered, "Ndodana may be an excellent geography teacher, but what does he know about our culture? Listen, people, we stick to our culture! The mission must cook and dish out enough food to fill us up and we still have leftovers."

"Come on, guys," Park pleaded. "We are refusing to see something that is out in the open like the private parts of a pig."

"It may be out in the open," Albert bellowed, "but how do we see it in this pitch dark night?"

Rowdy laughter filled the dormitory and the argument ended: Albert 3, Park 0.

Forty seven years later, the argument still rages in my head. Should we tamper with our culture to accommodate changing circumstances?

Nothing delighted me more than when in class we heard the shout: "Fire in the veld!" This was the only time Ndodana suspended classes. In a split second he transformed from a smiling gentle teacher into an energetic fire fighter.

The neck tie was yanked off and sleeves of his white shirt were rolled back. He barked instructions to staff, villagers and boys. In the veldt, he raced the tractor in all directions, mowing down the tall grass before the fire got there.

We always put out the fire before much harm was done. Ndodana would then go round, thank and shake hands with each fire fighter. In 1968, when I was at school, Ken Smith was our role model and he was loved by the local community. He left that year to move to the LMS secondary school at Moeding in Botswana.

Marieke Clarke comments:
Botswana (formerly the British High Commission Territory of Bechuanaland) became independent in September 1966 and urgently needed people qualified to work in the civil service and other professions. This problem had been caused by the shortage of educational facilities and the unwillingness of whites in senior positions in Bechuanaland to train African juniors. At the most, on Botswana's Independence Day, there were fewer than 30 university graduates among its approximately 535,000 black people. The situation with education and infra-structure illustrates the extent to

which the colonial government had neglected the (then) Bechuanaland Protectorate.[98]

WHAT WAS KENNETH SMITH'S EDUCATIONAL PHILOSOPHY?

Mzana Mthimkhulu remembers:

I recall that one of Ken Smith's favourite parables was that of The Good Samaritan[99]. In 1968 I was a member of the Puppet Club that Ken led. After we had made puppets, we went round to several homes in the evenings using the puppets to tell the parable. (The biggest crowd we got was at the home of Jeremiah Khabo)[100]. Kenneth would then teach/explain the meaning of the parable. He stressed that the biggest challenge a Christian faced was to love his enemies in the way that the Samaritan did.

The only time I recall Kenneth making a political comment was on Speech Day, 1968. He gave a summary of the previous year's 'O' level results in which he noted that one student, Wise Dube, had done well but could not get a place to do 'A' levels. Kenneth then commented that this was a 'disgrace to our country.'

---

[98] Quotation slightly edited from Williams, Susan, "Colour bar: the triumph of Seretse Khama and his nation" (Penguin Books, UK 2016)
[99] St Luke's Gospel, Chapter 10
[100] See chapter on Mr Khabo.

DOLLY DOREEN NCUBE (nee MOYO)

She entered Inyathi School in 1970.

I was born on 29th November 1955 at Ezinyangeni in Nkayi District. George and I were twins. Our father was Makhanda and our mother was Sidelile Ndebele. Ngutshana was my paternal grandfather, whose wife was Xotshiwe Dabengwa Ndlovu. Ngutshana was a soldier who belonged to the Elibeni ibutho[101] or Village in Ntabazinduna. Galu Mlotshwa was the Commander and Chief of the Iliba *ibutho*. We do not have concrete knowledge about Gugu, who is said to have been Ngutshana's father.

Like many people at Nkayi, we were evicted from ancestral land at Vizhe, which was close to Manyanga, NtabazikaMambo. In fact, we are the royal Moyos, the Dewas, also known as Vumabalanda. We had, after the arrival of the Ndebele, come under the *ibutho* known as Ujinga under the leadership of Mletshe Ndiweni, who was succeeded by his son Nkomo, whose sister Mahwe married King Lobhengula Khumalo. Nkalakatha Ndiweni was the chief who led our people to Ezinyangeni, following our eviction from Kenilworth, where we had settled after being evicted from Vizhe.

At Ezinyangeni we found many Nguni families, amongst whom was Makuni Mabhena, nationalist Welshman Mabhena's father. Evictees we found there had come from various places such as Inyathi, Bubi, Emakhandeni, Bulawayo and other places from the watershed. At the time, Ezinyangeni was a boarding school with a well-functioning hospital which was destroyed during the War of

---

[101] Conscription cohort

Liberation. There were white missionaries that served at the mission, notably Reverend Norman Clark, Reverend James Pelling. These were later succeeded by African clergy who included Reverend Joshua Danisa and Reverend Amos Mzilethi.

It was Reverend Mzilethi who, at the time he served at Ezinyangeni, lamented the evictions that had taken place. "Many people were moved to Shangani and elsewhere (by the white government regulations). This forced us to close down some of our schools and our church members were scattered. This shifting and re-shifting of people leads to a growing sense of insecurity, indifference to all efforts made for the development of Africans, bitterness, disillusionment and loss of confidence in the Government. This birth of an Anti-European feeling may have far- reaching repercussions not only for the future of the country, but on the work of Christian missions in general. The more vocal of our people contend that the Christian churches in our land failed to exert themselves to protect the interests of the weaker section of our Rhodesian community."

In my youthful days at Ezinyangeni, I herded goats, donkeys and cattle. This was at a time when hyenas were rampant and used to kill our livestock. We heard about frightening stories from earlier settlers but there were none during our time. I was also involved in milking my father's cows. These duties were normally reserved for boys and men, but I performed them. In addition to these male duties, my grandmother taught me how to weave sleeping and sitting mats using grass known as *inqodi*.

When time came for me to go to school, my father, who was church leader at Ezinyangeni, sent me to our school, which was built and run by the London Missionary Society (LMS). I enrolled for Sub-Standard A in 1962. The Head Teacher was Mothelesi from Botswana. The LMS had a strong presence in Botswana. Mothelesi came from Moeding College near Lobatsi, close to the border with South Africa. Other teachers at the school included the following: Lucy Siso (Mrs. Ndlovu), Mrs. Ndlovu (nee Mabhena, the mother of Professor Lindela Ndlovu who was to become Vice Chancellor of the National University of Science and Technology (NUST), July Nkomo and my brother Vayi Moyo. In 1967 I completed Standard 6.

I then enrolled for Form 1 at the Roman Catholic boarding school near Gwayi River known as Regina Mundi.[102] I got to the school in 1968. Here I met children of nationalists such as Joshua Nkomo and Stephen Jeqe Nkomo. Joshua Nkomo's children were Thandiwe Barbara and Ernest Thuthani, while Khanyisile Nkomo was Stephen Nkomo's daughter. These children of detainees had their school fees paid by Christian Care, in which Reverend Stephen Manguni played an important role. Reverend Elliot Dhlula, another clergyman in the Anglican Church, was also active in assisting the children of political detainees. At primary school, we had Landiso, the daughter of Welshman Hadane Mabhena.

While there were two classes each in Forms 1 and 2 at Regina Mundi, there was only one Form 3 class. That meant that some of us were not going to proceed to Form 3. Only Roman Catholic pupils were to proceed. Being a member of the LMS, I could not be taken to Form 3.

As a result, I spent the year 1969 at home and only proceeded to Inyathi Mission in 1970 where I attended for two years. The school Head at Inyathi Mission at that time was Mr Philip Symes whom we called Mboks. Other teachers included Robert Moyo, the Mathematics teacher, who was keen on athletics. I was an accomplished athlete who was trained by Robert Moyo. Murashiki, Mr Themba Nhlapo, Miss Hazel Barkham and Mrs Mothalife were

---

[102] " Queen of the World" in Latin. It refers to the Virgin Mary, Jesus's mother. MFC

some of the teachers at the school in my time. There were four sports houses, namely Thomas, to which I belonged, Sykes, Moffat and Rees.

During our time there were many students who were coming from Bulawayo. Some of us who hailed from Nkayi were not very much exposed to city life. When schools closed, our school truck took us directly to Nkayi.

At Inyathi Mission, on the other hand, urban influence was strongly felt. One day, two students were taken in by Inyathi police for indications and interrogation with regard to their political activities. Stephen Mpofu was one of them. In response, there was arranged what came to be known as the Battle of Ngwigwizi. Ngwigwizi is a river near the school that one crosses to get to the police camp at Inyathi.

The strike was fomented by the fact that Stephen and his colleague had been arrested by police. There were also grievances bordering on the welfare of teachers. The famed Battle of Ngwigwizi took place in 1970. Police became aware of our march on their camp. They waylaid us on the Ngwigwizi River. When we approached the river in the dark of the night, police fired warning shots into the air, we panicked, with some of us not having heard gunshots before. I was in Form 3 then. In the ensuing melee, one of the fleeing girls got seriously bruised in the legs.

Mrs. Mhlanga was our Boarding Mistress while MaNyoni, who was au fait with the history of Inyathi Mission[103], was girls' Matron. She tried to dissuade us from taking part in the impending Battle of Ngwigwizi. Stephen Mpofu and colleague were released from police custody the next morning and resumed lessons.

---

[103] Makhaza, who was killed by Ndebele forces in 1896 because he saved the lives of Rev and Mrs Bowen Rees, was a family member of MaNyoni. MFC

In 1971 I left Inyathi Mission and stayed home in 1972. The following year, 1973, I went to Bulawayo in search of a job. Success did not come my way. As a result, I became a temporary teacher in Silobela in the Midlands. I taught at three Roman Catholic schools: Melusi, where I met Father Winter who was based at Loreto Mission, and I also served stints at Fatima and St Dominic's. In 1976 I secured a place at the new Mkoba Teachers' College where we were pioneering students. Our Principal was Mr D. G. Griffiths who was later succeeded by Mr Kwidini. In 1978 I fell pregnant and left college. I was at home in 1979 and 1980. Principal Kwidini then arranged that I go to Bondolfi College in Masvingo, run by the Dutch Reformed Church (DRC). Once I qualified as a teacher, I went to teach at Magama Mission in Tsholotsho. I stayed there for only six months and left because of dissident activity. The dissidents used to knock on the doors of young girls demanding sexual favours. There was martial law and a dusk to dawn curfew. I could not bear it any more. The Rhodesian government soldiers pestered and accused us of supporting dissidents.

In 1986 I went to teach at the Cecil John Rhodes School (CJR) in Gweru where I strongly campaigned for the introduction of the IsiNdebele language. I succeeded. I was at the school from 1986 to 1996. I got legally married to Amson Ncube in 1982. When my husband went to head Plumtree High School, I transferred to Redfern in Plumtree town. There I stayed from 1997 to 2006. In 2007 I taught at Marula for just one year prior to moving to Bulawayo, where I served at Coghlan School for just one term in 2008. I joined the staff at Kumalo Primary School where I have remained to this day.

Amson and I have three children: two girls, Xolile and Lungisa and one boy, Makabongwe.

Interview by Pathisa Nyathi

HARRIET NCUBE (nee DUBE)
She entered Inyathi School in 1973.

I was born at St Luke's Hospital in the Lupane District of Matabeleland North in 1958. My father was Joel Dube and my mother was Dainah Dube (nee Ncube). There were eight of us in the family. I was the second born. I attended Mtupane Primary School in the Gwampa Valley from 1964 to 1970. Mr. Ken Moyo was the Head Teacher. Other teachers at the school included Mr Tshuma, Mr Sojila, Mr Mpofu, Miss Ncube, and Mr Nxumalo.

For my secondary education I went to Inyathi Mission in Bubi District. Some of my schoolmates were Obadiah Moyo, (See the chapter on him), Lucy Dube, Cephe Khumalo, Londiwe Dube, Ian Dube and Dubabantu. At the time I was at Inyathi Mission, the following were some of the teachers: Mr. Mpofu, Mr Ndebele, Mr. Robert Moyo, Mr. Ndlovu, Mr. Douglas Dube. I did the following subjects: English Language, Mathematics, English Literature, Geography, History, General Science and IsiNdebele. My interests outside the classroom were netball, reading and sewing.

Inyathi students were politically conscious. At one time police took away and detained some Form 4 students because of their political involvement. The Deputy Head at the time, Mr. Douglas Dube, was my uncle, who was known to be an activist in the Zimbabwe African People's Union (ZAPU). Naturally, I was picked up as a suspect. I was taken for interrogation by police at the nearby Inyathi Police Camp. Questioning lasted several hours. In 1974 I left Inyathi Mission.

From 1976 to 1977 I taught as a temporary teacher at Jotsholo Primary School in Lupane. There I taught Grades 2 and 5. I later transferred to Tshebetshebe Primary School, also in the same district, where I taught a Grade 3 class. I was also coaching the netball team at the school. I was at Tshebetshebe Primary School when the War of Liberation was getting hotter in Matabeleland North. One person sold out to the Rhodesian security forces. We were accused of supporting the Zimbabwe People's Revolutionary Army (ZPRA) guerrillas. All young ladies were picked up and severely tortured.

I was picked up at a road block on my way to Bulawayo. Ironically, I was the only person who was picked up from among several passengers on the bus. It dawned on me then that I was the target for the road block. The sort of torture I underwent may not be described in a book, save to say I was tortured big time. Electric currents were passed through our nipples, in an effort to make me confess to supporting ZPRA guerrillas. The soldiers wanted us to tell them where guerrillas had cached their arms. The truth was that we women prisoners did not know. When we pleaded ignorance, we courted the wrath of the soldiers, who subjected us to more torture and beatings. I resigned my fate to God.

I was detained at Lupane Police Station with a lady known as MaHadebe. Her husband, Mr. Dube, was a villager at the school where I taught and a Headmaster at some neighbouring school. At Lupane Police Camp, there was a policeman who seemed to be friendly and questioned me in a way that seemed to suggest he was sympathetic to me. He wanted to know more about my parents, whom he promised to alert about my presence at the camp. I was kept in a small cell.

One day, the same policeman was on night duty. He came to my cell. I was immensely terrified. A few days earlier MaHadebe, who was pregnant, had been taken away when she aborted as a result of torture. I was asked to go to the police charge office. The policeman was alone in the office. He sat on the table and I sat on a bench. All manner of thoughts raced through my mind. At midnight a Prisons truck arrived on the scene. The policeman smuggled me into the truck bound for Hwange, the Matabeleland North Police Headquarters in charge of Lupane Police Camp. "You are going to Hwange," said the policeman. I later learnt that there were plans to get rid of me that very night. I stayed in Hwange Women's Prison for just over a year before I was released with three other women, for lack of evidence in court. We had maintained that we were tortured to admit to the charges levelled at us.

My uncle Douglas Dube visited Zimbabwe just a few days after my release. He had emigrated to Botswana where he was Deputy Principal at Moeding College in Lobatse. We travelled together by train and duped the security personnel that I was going to work for him, more precisely to look after his sick wife. I had a passport which I had got while I was in Form 2, courtesy of my father. That is how I managed to get to Botswana, where I was declared a refugee.

Conditions for my stay in Botswana were that I report to immigration officials in Gaborone every week. I was receiving some allowance that was being given to refugees. That was the money that I used for transport. My stay with my uncle was also another nightmare. In Botswana, there were a number of Non Governmental Organizations (NGOs) that were keen to render some assistance to refugees. One day I went to report to the immigration office as usual and saw, on notice boards, several notices on available scholarships. I applied to some of them. Replies came in a couple of months. I was awarded a Phelps Stoke Fund Scholarship in the United States of

America. But I needed to sit a TOEFEL Test (Test of English as a Foreign Language). The second offer was a Soviet Scholarship where I was going to spend the first year learning the Russian language. I chose to go to the USA where I obtained my first Degree in Library Science at the Illinois State University. I also did some Physiotherapy courses in Atlanta, Georgia.

I returned home in 1984 and subsequently obtained a Master's Degree in Library and Information Science from the National University of Science and Technology (NUST). There was already a job waiting for me. I have been involved in a number of organizations since my return. I am active in the Zimbabwe Academic and Non-Fiction Authors' Association (ZANA). I serve on the National Executive Council of the Zimbabwe Library Association (ZIMLA-NEC). I am a Member of the Council for the Bulawayo Polytechnic Advisory Council and Chairperson of the Academic Committee.

While I am a Member of the Sectoral Board in the Division of Applied Science and Technology at the Bulawayo Polytechnic, I am also a Member in the Library and Information Science Department within the Faculty of Communication and Information at NUST. I am the Treasurer of the Matabeleland Reading Awareness Campaign (MRAC).

I got married but now I am a divorcee with three sons. When I gave birth to my second son in the USA, I kept the umbilical cord and brought it home to Zimbabwe with me. I am particularly keen on cultural issues and values and also on indigenous knowledge. My grandmother, who was my best friend, told me lots of stories and cultural knowledge.
Interview by Pathisa Nyathi

OBADIAH MOYO

Entered Inyati School in 1973

I CAME FROM A POLITICAL FAMILY: MY MOTHER WAS AN ACTIVIST

My mother, Laster Mpofu, was a political activist under the leadership of Welshman Mabhena[104]. She was on a number of occasions found by the Rhodesian police on the wrong side of the law.

The Mabhenas had their homestead at Zinyangeni and their neighbours were the Siso family, cousins to my mother. My mother's homestead was at Guwe, about 10kms south of the Mabhena homestead.

FORCED REMOVAL AND MY MOTHER'S RESISTANCE TO WHITE MINORITY RULE

My mother's family, the Mpofus, were forcibly removed from their fertile land in Bubi District, close to the Mambo Mountains (Intaba zika Mambo)[105] in the 1930s, when my mother was a baby. The family had to move because the Land Apportionment Act of 1930 came into force. So my mother and her parents had to move from fertile land to give way to white settlers.

The Mpofu family members were then settled at a thick forest, in present day Nkayi district, an area infested with tsetse flies. The bites of tsetse flies led to my mother's contracting the dreadful and incurable disease of sleeping sickness. My mother lived with this disease till she passed away in 2000.

---

[104] See Chapter on Welshman Mabhena.

[105] See Clarke, Marieke, "The Mambo Hills, Historical and Religious Significance" (amaBooks, Bulawayo, 2008)

This colonial history, and the brutality of the Rhodesian government towards the local people, fuelled my mother's hatred of the regime. In Welshman Mabhena, my mother found a leader of the resistance movement that fought any laws introduced by the regime.

In the 1950s to 1960s, when all families were asked to dip their cattle and take their children for immunisation injections against childhood diseases, my mother resisted such moves. She mobilised other youths and heaped sand in dip-tanks and prevented mothers taking their children for immunisation.

MY MOTHER'S COMMITMENT TO THE FREEDOM STRUGGLE CAUSED ME TO CONTRACT POLIO

In later years my mother explained to me how I contracted polio in 1959, at the age of three years. I contracted polio as a result of her political activism and her resistance to the white regime. Once, after being convinced by my grandmother to take me for vaccinations, my mother got wind that the police were hunting for her: as a result she abandoned the visit to the clinic.

WHY MY MOTHER SENT ME TO INYATHI SCHOOL

When in 1972 it was time for me to seek a secondary school place, my mother said that my first choice should be Inyathi Mission, the school where Welshman Mabhena went for his education. Luckily, I got a place at Inyathi.

Because of the physical impairments I suffered from polio, I was accompanied to Inyati School by my mother. I was one of very few students whose mother came with him using public transport. We started our journey at 5 o'clock in the morning in a donkey-drawn cart from the Dolahali area of Nkayi (in the Shangani Reserve) to Tohwe where we boarded a bus to Inyathi.

INYATHI STUDENTS JOIN THE
ACTIVE STRUGGLE FOR LIBERATION

My time at Inyathi School was during the height of the Liberation Struggle. A lot of us Inyathi students were from the rural areas. We understood the oppression that our own parents were going through, and the farming that they were trying to do in the barren lands of the Shangani Reserve.

In my first year at Inyathi, I became aware that in Rhodesia there was a two tier education system, one for whites called "A schools" that had better educational facilities. These A schools prepared whites to become bosses and leaders. Then there were the B schools for blacks that aimed at developing black students to become good employees/workers for the white Rhodesians.

This system and the poor conditions in our villages made us search for information about political parties such as the Zimbabwe African People's Union (ZAPU) and its military wing ZPRA.

My mother's activism, the leadership of Welshman Mabhena and the political awareness of the Shangani people, all this I shared with other students at Inyathi Mission. The discussions and sharing motivated us and gave hope that indeed the struggle for a free nation would one day be a reality. This made us work hard in our studies…with the hope that one day we shall be leaders in a free Zimbabwe. Armed with tools of education, we Inyathi students saw ourselves as liberators of our parents, who sold their cattle to ensure that we had a good education.

My own political baptism came when, as students, we started to research more about the Liberation Struggle and the men and women behind it. Welshman Mabhena, being from the Shangani Reserve and a former student at Inyathi Mission, became one of our heroes and role model. We called him Mawelishi.

Newspapers exposed us to some of the top figures in ZAPU.
During the weekends we students had access to a radio that was smuggled into our dormitories by one of the senior students. In the

evenings we tuned to Radio Zambia and listened to a ZAPU/ZPRA broadcast and got updates on the Liberation Struggle.

At Inyathi School we formed an underground ZAPU Link Group to exchange views and ideas on the Liberation Struggle. Also we received and shared information on the links for those willing and able to join the War of Liberation.

Many students left our school either soon after Form Four or in the middle of their studies to join the Liberation Struggle, and ZPRA, the political party of Mawelishi, was their destiny. One of my best school friends, class- and dormitory mate, joined ZPRA after Inyathi. I was keen to meet him after the end of the War of Liberation but heard, to my grief, that he got killed during the struggle.

When I was at college, to my surprise, I would get communications from some school-mates who had joined ZPRA. As a ZAPU Youth I kept in contact with the party up to the Unity Agreement with ZANU in 1987.

Among the various courses in Administration and Management of Non-Governmental Organisations that I successfully completed, I also attained the following:

- Diploma-Business Administration
- BA- Public Administration
- MA- International Relations

I hold an Honorary Doctor of Philosophy degree (Ph D) which was conferred by the National University of Science and Technology (NUST), Bulawayo. This was in recognition of my invention of the Donkey Drawn Mobile Libraries Concept and the establishment of a network of viable libraries in the rural areas.

In 1998 I was approached by some ZAPU leaders, including Welshman Mabhena, to contest the Nkayi constituency in the ZANU- PF primary elections for the position of Member of Parliament for Nkayi. Primary elections were held in 1999 and I won the ticket to represent ZANU-PF. I lost the election to the Movement for Democratic Change in the general elections of 2000.

In 2005 I was invited to contest the Nkayi constituency and won the ZANU-PF primary elections but lost in the general elections. In 2008 I left active politics to concentrate on the activities of the Rural Libraries and Resources Development Programme (RLRDP). My political activities, kindled at Inyathi School, in later life gave me a deeper understanding of the political thinking among the various groups in Zimbabwe.

O. N. THEMBA NHLAPO
Teacher at Inyathi School, later Head Teacher.

By *Marieke Clarke*
Friday 12th June, 1964.

The South African judge will declare the sentences for the Rivonia Trial prisoners: Nelson Mandela, Walter Sisulu, Govan Mbeki and their comrades. Most of the world is watching. So are many people at Inyathi School. Themba Nhlapo, a South African teaching IsiZulu, English and football, had a free teaching period. So he and Marieke Clarke agreed in advance that he would follow the news at home on his personal radio. Then he could report back as soon as possible whether the Rivonia heroes were going to live or die. Marieke was teaching, but some of her thoughts were on the drama at Pretoria, where the sentence would be pronounced.

Suddenly she saw Themba running across the football field from his house, waving his arms! He looked very happy. "It's life!" he called. The class that Marieke was teaching erupted with joy. The message went round the school that the ANC prisoners had life sentences, but at least the Rivonia Trial heroes were not going to die immediately.

Themba, a graduate of Fort Hare in South Africa, and Marieke became good friends at Inyathi School. She knew from her student days at Oxford, in the UK, about the African National Congress of South Africa and was glad to learn that Themba was a sympathiser. His wife Bongiwe, a nurse, was usually in South Africa so that their babies, born there, would be entitled to South African passports. In

Bongiwe's absence, Marieke would cook Sunday lunch for Themba. Sundays could be rather lonesome for single staff. [106]

The day came when police arrived unannounced to deport Marieke. As a policeman stood by Marieke at the Inyathi School staff room, she passed an address book containing certain addresses to Themba. The addresses were of organisations such as the Anti-Apartheid Movement in London. Marieke's personal addresses were in a different book. Themba hid the political address book in his lavatory (the houses for African staff at Inyathi School at that time had outside toilets) and posted it to his friend Stephen Mpashi, a writer who lived in Lusaka. Mr Mpashi posted Marieke's address book to her in the UK.

There was a gap of a couple of days between the first police visit and Marieke's removal from the School. This was because there was no aeroplane to take her from Bulawayo to Salisbury.

Finally she had to leave the place which had for 15 months been her home. Themba had the amazing courage to accompany her to Bulawayo[107]. He did this so she would have company and not be alone with the police, who finally drove in a separate car. As the car with Themba, the Maths teacher Mary Austin and Marieke left the Inyathi School campus, a guard of honour stood watch over them. This was organised by Zwelibanzi Mzilethi (See separate chapter) and the Invisible Black Stones. (See also photo below of Mary Austin)

---

[106] The other African graduate, Mr Kono Ndlovu, drove to Bulawayo at weekends to be with his family. His wife was, like Bongiwe a nurse. Quite often Marieke had a lift with Kono if she wanted to visit friends in the city.
[107] He could have been deported.

As the War of Liberation developed, white staff left Inyathi School and Themba Nhlapo became head teacher. He later held a highly responsible educational post in the city of Durban.

The friendship between the Nhlapos and Marieke continued. They visited her in Oxford. She stayed with them in their home in South Africa in 1996 and in 2009. In early 2017 in a telephone conversation, he gave Marieke permission to mention in this book their experiences at Inyathi School.

Mary Austin and her husband John Ayton, about 1989

MARIEKE CLARKE:

How I went to Southern Rhodesia

In 1936 or 1937 two liberal Protestant church ministers met at a Christian pacifist conference in the Netherlands. They were Alan Knott from the Congregational Church in Bishop's Stortford, Herts, England[108], and Douwe Faber from the Netherlands. They became good friends. Douwe told me when I grew up that he asked Alan Knott if he knew of any household in England where Douwe's daughter Titia (pronounced Teet-sha) could stay and perfect her English. Middle class girls in the Netherlands were expected to speak two or three languages[109] as well as their own: this was because the Dutch were and are a trading nation. Alan Knott replied that Titia could stay with him and his wife Grace to help care for their sons.

Through the Knott family and the Congregational Church, Titia came to know and fall in love with a handsome young Christian pacifist called Richard Clarke. They were married in a Dutch town hall in August 1939: Alan Knott took a leading role in the church service. Fifteen months later Titia died in childbirth with me, having suffered a catastrophic haemorrhage, the like of which our family doctor later told me he had never seen. I was brought up by close family friends as well as by my father's mother and sister, while my father earned our living.

---

[108] Bishop's Stortford was the birthplace of Cecil Rhodes, son of an Anglican parson. Nobody in my family circle had the slightest interest in Rhodes while I was a child.
[109] For example, German, French and English

I was selected to attend a free academic secondary school and then won a place at Somerville College, Oxford. The school had ensured that we students had a firm grounding in Current Affairs. Each year we had the chance to attend conferences of the Council for Education in World Citizenship (CEWC) in London. We learned at school about the iniquities of the apartheid system in South Africa and we learned a little about Southern Rhodesia.

My father ensured that I was reared and thoroughly trained as a Christian pacifist, by sending me to youth conferences of the Fellowship of Reconciliation. The FOR brought us up to date with all important issues of responsible citizenship: with my father and aunt, I was soon a member of the Campaign for Nuclear Disarmament. My closest school friend called me "politically precocious". In my family there was little alternative, as discussions about current affairs regularly took place over the dining table and my father and aunt attended meetings most evenings.[110]

The empowering atmosphere in my home, where my grandmother was a leader in her women's organisation, my father was a deacon in the church, and my aunt a distinguished solo singer, prepared me for activism in the wider society. I later became aware that my mother and her mother had also spoken in public in the Netherlands.

The Congregational Church continued to be an important factor in my life. When I was about 16, John Ferguson, then professor of Classics at Ibadan University, Nigeria,[111] preached at our church. He challenged those of us who could do so to teach in Africa for three years. It was a challenge I was keen to respond to.

---

[110] My grandmother was always at home to attend to me.
[111] Afterwards, head of the Selly Oak Colleges in Birmingham

Just before I sat my A level exams, my aunt paid for me to attend a weekend Christian Action conference in Cambridge. It was probably then that I joined the Anti-Apartheid Movement, of which I remained an enthusiastic member till South Africa's first democratic elections in 1994.

At Oxford, 1959-62, I read history, a discipline that I love to practise. But at that time we university students had almost no choice of syllabus topics and the course did not engage my emotions. I felt no sense of purpose in the work, except to gain a respectable degree. But lack of purpose in work was no problem to me. My father and my aunt had had little emotional engagement with their paid work. Their sense of purpose was satisfied by the many meetings they attended in their spare time as well as their Congregational Church.

For me, the best aspect of Oxford University life was the limitless choice of committees that I could join. I became an office bearer of the Joint Action Committee Against Racial Intolerance. [112] One of JACARI's activities was to administer a scholarship to enable a black South African to study at Oxford University. The two I knew were Jeppe Mei and Edward Mafethe. I remember weeping with another JACARI committee member when Jeppe finished his degree and left Oxford.

Through JACARI, I met a challenging group of distinguished white South African students, all male except for Katherine Reeves, the daughter of Ambrose Reeves, former Bishop of Johannesburg. In 1961, while I was at university, and the notorious Treason Trial was still in progress, 69 people were killed by the South African police at Sharpeville. JACARI played its part in successfully campaigning for

---

[112] JACARI existed for two purposes: (1) To arouse among members of the University an interest in the problems of race relations in the Commonwealth by spreading reliable information...and (2) To find constructive ways of expressing a dislike of racial discrimination

South Africa to be expelled from the British Commonwealth. I was on the demonstration in London.

Martin Legassick was one of the South African students. [113] He was then Overseas Representative for the National Union of South African Students while studying Theoretical Physics. Through his NUSAS work, he met people in the South African African National Congress like the IsiZulu scholar and poet Mazizi Kunene, who was then the ANC representative in Europe.

In my third year at Oxford, Martin learned that I was returning to the university to do a Diploma in Education at Oxford while he would be working for Finals. He asked me to give him administrative support with his NUSAS work, which I gladly agreed to do. The Diploma in Education was relatively undemanding, after an Oxford Honours degree, and I was delighted to have extra work to do that gave me a sense of purpose. But I did have the opportunity in my Dip. Ed. Studies to choose a special essay topic and I wrote on South African education. Through Martin Legassick and NUSAS, I made some of my best Southern African white friends.

I used my room in Oxford for small committee meetings. It was there that Terence Ranger, recently deported from the University College of Rhodesia and Nyasaland, came to talk to JACARI in the spring of 1963. My friendship with him lasted till his death in January 2015.

As my rich fourth Oxford year came to an end (in July 1963) I saw an advertisement, in the *Times Educational Supplement*, for a history teacher with the London Missionary Society[114] at Moeding College in what would soon be Botswana. I was seeking to follow John Ferguson's advice by teaching at a school in Africa. Katherine Reeves's father, the former Bishop Reeves, had advised me to seek a

---

[113] Martin Legassick (1940-2016) later became Professor of History at the University of the Western Cape, South Africa.
[114] The LMS was the missionary society of the Congregational Church,

job in Bechuanaland or Swaziland rather than elsewhere in Southern Africa.

I asked Alan Knott, the Congregational minister who had introduced my parents, to be my referee. He had worked from 1950 to 1954 at the LMS tertiary institution Tiger Kloof in the Tswana cultural area of South Africa. But Tiger Kloof was closed in 1955 under apartheid legislation. Moeding College was opened in 1962 for Batswana students in what was soon going to be independent Botswana. The job seemed to be designed for me.

But while LMS staff in London were briefing me in preparation for my departure to Botswana, they said they were, instead, going to send me to Inyathi School in Matabeleland. I protested, but was confronted with the choice: "It's either Inyathi or you have no job with us."

It is instinctive to me to be a member of a political party. Shortly before I left the UK in August 1963, I joined the Labour Party, of which I remained a member till the late 1990s.

TO INYATHI SCHOOL

The induction that the Inyathi principal Kenneth Maltus Smith and his wife Mavis gave me was undoubtedly the best I ever had for any job. They even told me to bring warm bedroom slippers so that I should be prepared for the chilly winter nights in central Matabeleland.

The first weekend I spent with the Smiths, and I then moved for one month to the house of Mary Austin, the Maths teacher. This also was to become a lifetime friendship and we met regularly till she died in the UK in November 2015.

After this supportive start at Inyathi, I was helped to move into a very attractive two-bedded modern bungalow with a verandah. There was a fairly modern kitchen (with a rather slow electric cooker and a fridge) and a modern bathroom with an indoor lavatory and hot running water. What luxury in a third world country!

The one drawback was that these teachers' houses were about 200 metres' distance from each other and there was no means of attracting attention. 22 years old, a woman, and having always lived in a densely populated area, most recently in a family house with two or three other lodgers, I was at first terrified of the quiet and isolation.[115] (The only telephone on the mission station was in the school office 20 minutes' walk from my home. Cell phones did not exist for many years after my time at Inyathi School.) Gradually, however, I became accustomed to the quiet, and realised that this was a very safe place.

I did make enquiries as to whether I could find a puppy to keep me company. But the principal's family warned me that all dogs locally were trained to attack Africans, so I should have to learn to live without a dog. This was perhaps the first practical way in which I realised that life at the Inyathi mission station was a world apart from white society just outside the gate.

A final touch to make my home was a cat. A dog was negotiable, but I can hardly live without a feline companion. Mary Austin's cat Alpha had produced a litter of kittens. I took the youngest, a beautiful tabby, and asked various friends what to call him. Martin Legassick, now at the Institute of African Studies at the University of Ghana, Legon, wrote suggesting Afrika Mayibuye, (Africa, let it return!) and that is what I called my kitten.

When in later months the Rhodesian police started to open and read my letters, they must have been surprised that this character Afrika Mayibuye shared my home. For, as early as 1925, the Secretary-General of the South Africa African National Congress had suggested "Immediate steps be taken to register the (ANC) Constitution, Nkosi Sikelel'i Afrika (God save Africa), the hymn of the ANC, and Mayibuye Afrika." Operation Mayibuye was the name of the draft strategy plan of the ANC's armed wing's

---

[115] My second stepmother, Jo Cox Clarke, when looking at photos of my home at Inyathi, gasped at the isolation.

Umkhonto we Sizwe that was found in July 1963 when South African police raided the Rivonia farm outside Johannesburg.

Politics were a reality inside as well as outside the school at which I taught. Many if not most of my students had been victims of a Southern Rhodesian state-initiated and conducted programme of institutional violence in the form of forced evictions. [116] In order to implement the 1930 Land Apportionment Act, Africans living and farming on fertile "white" land, for example on the watershed on which Harare and Bulawayo stand, were forcibly removed to the Reserves. The Shangani Reserve, a couple of hours' drive in a modern fast car to the north of Inyathi School, was one such "dumping ground".

The deaths and hardships which resulted from being forcibly abandoned in the disease-ridden wilderness were built into the evictees' collective historical memories. To quote the distinguished chief Sivalo, whose chieftaincy had moved to Nkayi by 1910[117]:

"We were around Bulawayo... This land (at Nkayi) was land for wild animals. We never liked this part of the country. We were forcibly moved. Up to now we don't like this place." I had many extremely angry students in my classes. This book describes some of their experiences.

Moreover, black Zimbabweans whom I knew and taught daily, even those who had only the vaguest knowledge of international affairs, could not help but be aware of current African affairs. Zambia would be independent in a matter of months. I was lucky enough to

---

[116] Alexander, J., McGregor, J, and Ranger, T: *Violence and memory:100 years in the 'Dark forests' of Matabeleland* (James Currey, Heinemann, David Philip & Weaver Press, 2000) p. 46 seq.

---

[117] Chief Sivalo, at a meeting of the chiefs' committee at Nkayi, 1993.

spend the first weekend of its freedom on the Zambian side of the Victoria Falls with some colleagues.

Teaching English and History to politically aware students was a delight to me, and kept me alert. Very fortunately, as this book shows, there was in the school a remarkable culture of free speech, totally unlike the atmosphere outside.

My family in England helped with the students' political education by sending the highly regarded weekly newspaper "the Observer" from the UK: the students read the paper avidly[118].

Staff at Inyathi School were expected not only to teach a full five day a week timetable but also to undertake School Improvement. This seemed a lot of work, since all preparation and marking had to be done in one's free time. But I had the huge joy in School Improvement, early on Saturday mornings, of running the school library, which had hardly any money but boasted an original drawing of King Lobhengula. I did my best, with very little cash, to build up the library stock.

Asked by the headmaster, I offered to run a Current Affairs Club, which was I believe the most popular organised evening activity in the school. The solid background given me by my family, school and Oxford University supported me: I loved the evening encounters with the students at the Current Affairs Club.

The school radio did its bit by breaking down during my stay at Inyathi School. There was no money to repair or replace it. With permission from the headmaster, I entertained at my house every weekday evening any interested senior boys who wanted to listen to the news on my radio. I deeply regret now that I neglected to interact adequately with the girls outside the classroom. Probably I thought that they were the responsibility of the boarding mistress

---

[118] In May 2018, in an Oxford seminar, the publisher James Currey described "the Observer" in the 1960's as "an outstanding source of information on the new Africa." The editor at the time was David Astor and Colin Legum was a contributor.

MaNyoni and of Mary Austin, who worked with her and lived near the boarding house.

As a Labour Party member in England, I was aware that I should join a trade union. I was soon introduced to Jeremiah Khabo, a local leader, LMS church activist and leader of the Rhodesian African Teachers' Union.[119] I joined the local branch of the ATU and, some time later, so did Mary Austin, who became its treasurer.

Some of my friends at Oxford had studied Anthropology, and my Dutch relatives were all fluent linguists, so I knew the importance of learning local languages. I determined to try to learn some isiNdebele. In the early months of my stay, I went regularly to the home of the beloved Inyathi Church minister, Rev Amos Mzilethi, for language lessons.[120] I found the language beautiful but very difficult. Moreover, I only heard it at church service on Sunday morning, since school students were supposed to speak only English on campus. Umfundisi (as we called him= Teacher) was himself extremely busy, especially with a new translation of the Bible into IsiNdebele. I did struggle through the two primers for infants' schools, but not much further.

Long school holidays gave me the opportunity to travel beyond Bulawayo. In the spring holiday of 1964, I went to a multi- racial work camp run by the Quakers Stanley and Margaret Moore of the Salisbury Christian Action Group. Margaret Moore was a ZAPU activist. Participants worked according to their strength and skill: race was an irrelevance. At last one was part of a large group of people who made friends regardless of their colour. At the camp I met a congenial African man, Percy Kandaswaswika, whom I later learned had been a friend of Terence Ranger, when he was teaching at the University College in Salisbury.

---

[119] See chapter on Mr Khabo.
[120] His wife Elizabeth was the sister of the distinguished educationalist and published author Peter Mahlangu.

Percy and I had a couple of dates together. We went to the rural wedding of a friend of his. The only problem was that he was not admitted to cafes along the road, so I had to buy cool drinks and take them out to the car. Less pleasant was a date with Percy in an urban setting, where we felt the hostility of especially white men towards a white woman in the company of an African. In one store, white men followed us threateningly while Percy and I dodged around counters.

In November 1964, suddenly police came to deport me. As Mary Austin, accompanied by the IsiZulu teacher, Themba Nhlapo, (see separate chapter) drove me out of the school grounds behind a police car, the Shangani Advancing Students' Association and the Black Stone Movement formed a guard of honour. [121]

I found it amazing that the Rhodesian police regarded me as so dangerous. When Terence Ranger and his wife Shelagh Ranger were being deported from Salisbury, they had two weeks to leave the country. I had 48 hours and that was longer than the police had originally planned, because they had to wait for a scheduled plane to take me from Bulawayo to Salisbury. Once I was on the plane, I realised how lucky I had been, living in a quiet rural area among congenial people. On the plane I was sitting next to the daughter of Joshua Nkomo's lawyer Leo Baron (brother of Jacob Bronowski [122].)The brave Baron family, living among white people, had been threatened with violence at their home because of Leo's work.

My father and stepmother Ursula Davies Clarke met me from Heathrow airport. During the next weeks I was teaching near my home. But meanwhile, Ambrose Reeves, the former bishop of Johannesburg, took me to the London office of the African National Congress of South Africa. The staff introduced me to ZAPU officials in London. Interviews with numerous journalists were arranged and I was able to get excellent coverage for my views of what was happening in Matabeleland.

---

[121] J Z Mzilethi, pers. comm
[122] British mathematician and historian, Author of "The ascent of man".

After some months working in London, I found a permanent job at Oxfam Education Department in Oxford. In spring 1968 I had the huge good fortune to find the beautiful rented flat at 5a Crick Road where I still live. While I was sitting among the packing cases, my first visitors were Umfundisi and Mrs Mzilethi (Mahlangu) from Inyathi. Umfundisi was in Oxford to talk at a small meeting about the struggle for land in Zimbabwe, which he did very effectively and with great passion.

Our affection for each other was undiminished after 14 years apart. Mrs Mzilethi asked me with great sadness, "Did you have guns in your house?" I assured her that, contrary to what she had apparently been told, I had as a pacifist of course had no guns in my house.

In 1971, I had the great privilege of welcoming J. Zwelibanzi Mzilethi (see separate chapter) to spend Christmas at Crick Road. And so the circle of friends at Inyathi and further afield in Matabeleland began to meet again. Robson Silitshena, from Nkayi, who had been in my Form 4, kept in close touch with me in those years. He did a Ph D in Geography at Sussex University and went to work in the University of Botswana at Gaborone in Botswana. After a career move back to Zimbabwe, he suddenly got ill and died quite young. This was a tragedy for me.

In early 1988 I attended an Oxford conference on Africa and once more met Terence Ranger. He told me that he had been appointed professor at Oxford University and would shortly be moving there. This was very exciting news. I attended his seminars and began to think of research work that I should like to do on Zimbabwean history. Thanks entirely to the collegiate atmosphere in Terry's research group, I found a wide range of new scholar friends. I also joined the Britain Zimbabwe Society and was an office bearer for several years.

Paid by Oxfam, in early 1989 I returned to Matabeleland. For my very imaginative and generous manager at Oxfam, Jane Holliday, asked if I would like to go to Zimbabwe to assess whether two major

Oxfam-funded projects should receive second instalments of European Union money. I was overjoyed and gladly accepted.

The first night I spent in Matabeleland in the Bulawayo home of my old Trade Union Chief, Jeremiah Khabo. He drove me to Inyathi, where the funeral would be held of MaNyoni, who, under the direction of Mary Austin, had supervised the girls in the Inyathi boarding house.

That return to Inyathi is etched into my memory, with the funeral held in the open air to the scent of thyme and the glorious unaccompanied singing. Umfundisi conducted the service. Afterwards, I took the opportunity of asking him a question. In Oxford I had been reading David Lan's book "Guns and rain: Guerrillas and Spirit Mediums in Zimbabwe"[123]. So I asked Umfundisi whether there were spirit mediums at Inyathi whom I should visit to announce that I had returned after 25 years.

"We have no spirit mediums at Inyathi," he replied. "As you know, there are shrines at the Mambo Hills. Christians and non- Christians go there." This piece of information was the starting point of one of my most interesting research projects.[124]

After the funeral, I stayed a couple of days with my dear friends Thandiwe and Enoch Bhebhe. No longer were there ridiculous and threatening laws to stop friends staying together. I had come back to my former African home.

By 1989 some of my closest Zimbabwean friends were senior Local Government Officers. It is given to few deportees, I think, to be removed by the police at the age of 23 and to return a quarter of a century later to stay in the house of the chief local government officer of the same area. That was my singular good fortune. My dear friend and best correspondent Jack Nhliziyo was now District

---

[123] Published James Currey, London; University of California Press, 1985.
[124] "Mambo Hills: historical and religious significance" by Marieke Clarke, with an introduction by Pathisa Nyathi, ('amaBooks, Bulawayo 2008)

Administrator at Inyathi. (See chapter on Jack Nhliziyo). The house and offices that I had regarded with distaste, as of the occupying forces, was now my host's home. He, his lovely warm wife Molly, a driver and I drove all over Bubi District to see the plans for development now that Unity had come.

The most important visit we made was to Queen Lozikeyi Dlodlo's grave[125]. As soon as Jack told me that he was planning to establish a Heroes' Acre there, I began to think of writing her story.

Jack's manager was J. Z. Mzilethi, to whom I had taught Latin in Form Two. He was Provincial Administrator of Matabeleland North and was, I thought, making a brilliant job of it. While I was in Bulawayo, I stayed with him and his wife Joyce. He said I could go anywhere in his province, but not to Nkayi: this was still too unsettled for me to visit.

One friend who contributed greatly to the study of Queen Lozikeyi was Dr Ioan Bowen Rees. In 1992, I could not afford to visit Zimbabwe, so I spent my August holiday reading in libraries. I chose to read the archives and letters of missionaries at Inyathi Mission from the time of King Lobhengula's flight onwards. The names of the missionary Bowen Rees and Queen Lozikeyi stood out in the LMS files. In 1993, I gave a paper at BZS Research Day in which I mentioned Bowen Rees. A few days later, Terry Ranger approached me smiling with a letter from his old college friend Ioan Bowen Rees.

Ioan, recently retired from being Chief Executive officer of the county of Gwynedd in North Wales, and a passionate Welsh nationalist, wanted to write his grandfather Bowen Rees's biography: he asked for Terry's help. This request was delegated to me and I worked closely with Ioan from then onwards till his death in 1999.

---

[125] Queen Lozikeyi Dlodlo was senior queen of King Lobhengula Khumalo. She was the intellect behind the massive 1896 War of the Red Axe, also known as Umfazo 2.

But Ioan had also sent Terry a handful of photographs that his grandparents took of Queen Lozikeyi. That provided the final push to my project. I had the title, which was to be "A very dangerous and intriguing woman", I had the photos. I just had to write the book.

I thought that, as I was by now committed to substantial research on Matabeleland, it was about time to try again to work at the language. I had the great good fortune to join with JoAnn McGregor and have lessons given by Millius Palayiwa Ncube[126]. By that time, however, I was too busy with my daily work at Oxfam (I was scheduled to go to North India where I needed to speak some Hindi) to be able to continue the isiNdebele lessons, and I regret that I have not resumed them since.

Since 1994 I have had the great privilege of working with Pathisa Nyathi. Together we research, interview, write up and publish the history of Matabeleland. Long may our collaboration continue!

Thanks to Rev. Kenneth Maltus Smith (who passed in 2015) for crucial information about Tiger Kloof and Moeding College.

---

[126] Another former Inyathi student.

MARIEKE CLARKE:
Rhodesia: To be prohibited

By Marieke Clarke
The original article was published in the Economist in London on 19th December 1964.

I was declared a prohibited immigrant of Rhodesia on 4th November after teaching for 15 months at Inyathi Secondary School. Though convinced that a transfer to democratic rule should come immediately, I had taken no part in politics while I was in Rhodesia; I had not attended any political meeting, I had not even written a letter to a Rhodesian newspaper[127]. I attended only three public meetings: one of these was a meeting at Mpopoma in Bulawayo of the Southern Rhodesian Teachers' Association. This is the only non-racial teachers' organisation in Rhodesia (but I was the only white among 300 Africans at that meeting.) The other two meetings were of Christian Action in Salisbury.[128]

This book shows that there was by Rhodesian standards a very liberal atmosphere at Inyathi Secondary School, at least till the end of 1964. With the full agreement of our head teacher, Kenneth Maltus Smith, I was able to share with the students my copy of the well-known left-of –centre weekly British newspaper **The Observer.** Moreover, when the school radio broke down shortly after I arrived, the principal allowed male students to come to my home in the evenings to listen to BBC broadcasts.[129] This offered the opportunity for rich friendships to develop between me and young men such as Jack Nhliziyo, J. Z. Mzilethi and Robson Silitshena. All these friendships have immeasurably enriched my life. I hope the book shows this.

---

[127] I had written many letters to British MPs at Westminster telling them of the situation in Matabeleland North.
[128] Christian Action was a non-racial organisation which, among other activities, ran non-racial camps where everyone worked according to their physical or other skills.
[129] Girls were staying in a special hostel far from the classrooms.

The first suggestion that I was in a particularly exposed position came when I was away from the school in the school holidays. I was trailed walking with an African man friend, whom I had met through Christian Action. I had become used to being stared at by whites who saw me with Africans in public, but this time two white youths followed us for over half an hour while we went in and out of shops and a library. In August 1964, my letters began to arrive more irregularly than usual; after that time, at least six of them never arrived at all.

On November 4th two plain- clothes policemen and an immigration officer[130] told me I was a prohibited immigrant; no reason was given and I was informed that there was no appeal. My house was thoroughly searched and all my private letters read. Three African National Congress pamphlets from South Africa, including Chief Luthuli's speech at the Nobel peace prize ceremony at Oslo, were confiscated.

The headmaster and staff of my school sent a request to the Rhodesian government that I should be allowed to stay three weeks until the 61 students I was preparing for public examinations had written their papers. But on November 6th I was deported.

I was very well supported as I left the school. Students led by J Zwelibanzi Mzilethi (See separate chapter) organised a guard of honour as I was driven asway. The IsiZulu teacher Mr ON T Nhlapo and the Maths teacher Miss Mary Austin, close friends of mine, drove in the car with me to Bulawayo while the policemen travelled in another vehicle.[131] Some students, for instance Jack Nhliziyo, came to the airport to see me leave.

---

[130] One of these men was from Abingdon near Oxford, UK. This fact illustrates the close collaboration between the then political police in the UK and Southern Africa.

[131] It was extremely brave of these two colleagues to make themselves conspicuous as my friends. Mr Nhlapo was and is a South African, Miss Mary Austin, who passed in 2015, was then British. They could have been deported too.

In Bulawayo I was five times fingerprinted, escorted by plain-clothes police to the bank and allowed, theoretically, to move freely till my aeroplane left. Mr Nhlapo, Mary Austin and I spent much of that time in the Centenary Park. Two white men closely watched us. One of the policemen later accompanied me on the aeroplane to Salisbury.

At Salisbury I was met by yet another plain-clothes policeman, and prevented from greeting four of the six friends[132] who had come to say goodbye. I was kept from the press, and my possessions were thoroughly searched. There was no witness with me during most of the search.

To me my deportation meant the end of a dream to teach in an African secondary school in southern Africa. To my students, whose exams were due to start on 23rd November, my deportation meant that the 28 young people to whom I was teaching English Language, English Literature, History and Latin at Cambridge Certificate Level lost their teacher at the most critical time. The 34 students whom I was preparing for the Junior Certificate may even have suffered more, for they were less mature. I was not replaced: this would have been impossible at such short notice.

In 2017 Marieke Clarke slightly edited and expanded the original article

FRIENDS IN BULAWAYO WHO SUPPORTED MARIEKE.

The work at the school was fascinating and demanding. But I was in my early twenties and single. There were no recreational facilities at Inyathi Mission. My stay in Rhodesia was immeasurably enriched by three hostesses in Bulawayo.

Because of the Land Apportionment Act[133], I could unfortunately stay only with white friends. One household I visited often,

---

[132] For example, from Christian Action
[133] The Land Apportionment Act sought to separate the races and confine the Africans to poorer and less land. Meanwhile the white people occupied a larger

especially in the early months, was of young white South African liberals from Cape Town. I had been introduced to them through the National Union of South African Students, which had members studying in Oxford.

The husband was a doctor, while the wife was a teacher and a fine artist. Their beautiful flat was a delight to my eyes, accustomed to the mostly dull pictures displayed on mission stations. These friends had transport and took me on picnics to the Matobo Mountains with other young professionals.

Unfortunately their friends, mostly junior doctor colleagues of the husband, invariably regarded me as a Communist[134] and "beyond the pale" socially. Conversations would start: "What's a pretty girl like you doing teaching munts[135] out there in the bush? Why don't you get a job teaching (white students)" in town?" I would cringe at their racist language.

I would explain that I had come from the UK specifically to teach in an African school. Within seconds I would be dismissed as not worth talking to. The only exception I remember was a man who tried hard to get into the bed I was assigned to sleep in: my hostess had to take extreme measures to get him out of it.

This couple left Rhodesia for the UK late in 1964 to advance the husband's career, but my friendship with the wife resumed in London and lasted for many years.

My other regular hostess in Bulawayo was also a South African. She was Hilary Flegg Mitchell, in her early forties, a politically radical medical sociologist and close friend of the Liberation Movement

---

acreage of more fertile land. This Act was a disempowering measure driven by deep-seated racial bigotry, hatred and greed.
[134] Any white person who did not agree with Rhodesian settler politics was liable to be regarded as a Communist.
[135] This was a term of disgust misusing the Ndebele word "umuntu" to refer to black people. Schools in Rhodesia were segregated by the colour of the students.

heroes Joe Slovo and Ruth First. Nelson Mandela himself had visited Hilary when he passed through Ghana in 1962.

I was introduced to Hilary through a contact I made at Oxford University. Hilary was based at Mpilo Hospital working towards a Ph D. studying cancer in the Bulawayo area: Bulawayo had been selected as the Africa Centre for the World Health Organisation because of the quality of its medical services.

Hilary became a role model to me and a hugely important mentor. She introduced me to feminism and convinced me that married women should do paid productive work outside the home. She took me to films in Bulawayo and helped me to relax in a politically congenial environment. She often stressed that Rhodesian white people were more racially prejudiced than South Africans- or perhaps one could say that in South Africa there were more white people who thought it normal to have African and Indian friends. I remember that Hilary occasionally referred to "Horrid white Rhodesians".

In 1963 Hilary, a widow, had married Professor J. Clyde Mitchell of the University College of Rhodesia and Nyasaland. She left Bulawayo to join Clyde in Salisbury shortly before I was deported. A few months later, they moved for his work to Manchester in the UK.

Hilary and I never lost touch, and, a few years later, both the Mitchells and I met up again in Oxford when Clyde came to work at Nuffield College. Hilary died very young of mesothelioma in 1976.

A third friend in Bulawayo, but not a hostess, was Patricia Battye (1920-2016). She went to Bulawayo in 1956 and worked for 25 years as a social worker with the Bulawayo African Affairs Department. Original, independent and fearless, ("I like to be where the action is".) Pat mixed as freely as was then possible with people of all social backgrounds. What I valued particularly was that Patricia took me and another young British visitor to World's View in the Matobo

Mountains. This sort of trip was a big treat to young single people working hard in fairly isolated settings such as Inyathi.

I lost contact with Patricia when I was deported.[136] But we resumed our friendship in 2001 when I was researching the life of Ramanbhai Naik, a Bulawayo business man who supported ZAPU members including Welshman Mabhena (see Joshua M. Mpofu's chapter). Patricia and I enjoyed years of rich friendship, particularly at Pat's retirement home in Suffolk, UK. This friendship was greatly enhanced by our shared love of Bulawayo.

MARIEKE'S RETURN TO BULAWAYO, EARLY 1989

Scene: a bank. I panicked. "They're going to lock me up," I declared loudly. Terror of the Rhodesian police, suppressed for 25 years, swept over me. The black woman bank clerk smiled at me indulgently: "Madam, things have changed," she said with a large grin. I realised then that Rhodesia had indeed become Zimbabwe.

The bank clerk had asked me: "Where are you staying?" as I needed to cash some money. And I had answered, without thinking: "Block 50, Number 172 Gampu Avenue, Mpopoma North." In 1963/4 it would have been a criminal offence, under the Land Apportionment Act, for me to stay in an African home.[137] Now I was a guest of Jack and Molly Nhliziyo. (See chapter on Jack Nhliziyo).

The Unity Accord in December 1987 had at last made it safe to visit Western Zimbabwe. Oxfam, my employer since 1965, had paid for me to return to assess two large projects[138] for renewed European

---

[136] I could not phone Patricia or any other friends when I was deported. The reason was that the only telephone at Inyathi School was in the school clerk's office. Moreover, the Inyathi School telephone line was a party line shared with a number of neighbouring white farmers. From the time they acquired their land after Conquest, these men were opposed to the African-friendly London Missionary Society. Mobile phones did not reach Zimbabwe for many years.

[137] See Chapter on Jack Nhliziyo.

[138] The Zimbabwe Project, supporting development work with ex combatants, and the Organisation of Rural Associations for Progress.

Union funding. I decided to combine the Oxfam work (which was successful) with visits to Inyathi and to the former Inyathi students with whom I was still in touch.

When I knew that I was returning to Zimbabwe, I asked Jack Nhliziyo if I could visit him and his family. His wife Molly (MaNgwenya) was with me at the bank. I stayed some time with them in their home at Mpopoma and some time with them at Inyathi.

For Jack Nhliziyo was now District Administrator of Bubi District: he worked from the official house at the government camp at Inyathi. The colonial district commissioner had deported me in 1964: on my return to Inyathi in 1989, it gave me great pleasure to move almost immediately into the guest room at the DC's old home to visit Jack and Molly.[139]

I stayed on that trip also with Zwelibanzi Mzilethi, (see separate chapter) his wife Joyce and their family. Zwelibanzi was now Provincial Administrator of Matabeleland North and Jack's manager. I also stayed with my former trade union chief, Jeremiah Khabo (see chapter on him), and his family. I travelled to Botswana to visit Dr Robson Silitshena, whom I had taught and known well at Inyathi. He had gained a Ph D at Sussex University in the UK and we kept up our friendship for a number of years. He was a leading light in the Department of Environmental Studies in the University of Gaborone and later moved to Africa University at Mutare. He died far too young in 2005.

INYATHI TEACHERS SUPPORT THEIR DEPARTED COLLEAGUE

When Marieke Clarke was removed from Inyathi School on 6th November 1964, she had solid support from her colleagues inside and outside the school.

---

[139] My first nights back at Inyathi were spent with friends I had made through the LMS church at Inyathi, Enoch and Thandiwe Bhebhe. Thandiwe has passed away but in 2017 Enoch and I met again.

We reproduce here documents that reflect this.

INYATHI TEACHER DEPORTED BY GOVERNMENT[140]

Miss Marieke Clarke, 24 year old high school mistress at Inyathi Secondary School, has been deported by the Rhodesian Government. She left Bulawayo last night for England, two days after she had been served with a deportation order.

Miss Clarke, who arrived in Rhodesia a year ago to take up a teaching appointment at Inyathi, (taught) English and History (and Latin) up to Form Four. The Principal, Rev K.M. Smith, said the deportation order was served on Miss Clarke on Wednesday, but no reasons were given.

An Immigration Department official confirmed in Bulawayo yesterday that Miss Clarke was being deported. Asked for the reasons for the order, he said: "She will be in a better position to tell you. I cannot."

Miss Clarke, who was a staunch member of the (Southern Rhodesian Teachers' Association) was well respected by members of her profession in Matabeleland.

A TELEGRAM

Immediately the news of her deportation was received in the City, the Matabeleland Regional Council of the (SRTA) sent a telegram to the president, Mr C G Msipa, asking him to make direct representations to the Governor for the association. The regional chairman, Mr T. N. Ncube, said "We have sent a telegram to the president asking him to make representations to the Governor on behalf of Miss Clarke. We are very much perturbed, but we do not know what has happened and why she has been deported."

---

[140] This appeared on the front page of *the Bulawayo Chronicle* on 7th November 1964. Marieke Clarke has made a few corrections (usually indicated by brackets).

Mr Smith said he was very sorry to lose Miss Clarke, and he had not been able to replace her. When Miss Clarke arrived at Salisbury airport last night, officials prevented the Press from interviewing her.

LETTER FROM INYATHI SCHOOL STAFF

To the Honourable I.D. Smith

Inyathi School
To the Governor
Private Bag J. 17
To the Minister for Internal Affairs, Salisbury
Bulawayo

Dear Sir,

11th November 1964

On Wednesday. November 4th, at Inyathi Mission, an Immigration official and two plain clothes detectives served on Miss Marieke Cambridge Faber Clarke an order declaring her to be a prohibited immigrant. She was given three days to leave Rhodesia.

Miss Clarke was a teacher at the Inyathi School and was teaching one class for the Rhodesia Junior Certificate and another class in three subjects for the Cambridge Overseas School Certificate Examination. These examinations commence on November 23rd.

It is with the gravest concern that we, her colleagues at this school view an action which has deprived 61 students of their teacher at a vital stage in their studies, and which is likely seriously to jeopardise their chances of success in examinations which play an extremely significant role in their lives.

A request for a stay of execution was made on the above grounds, but was rejected. At no stage has any reason been given for the deportation of Miss Clarke, and enquiries have met with a blunt refusal to present any. In view of these events and the hardship consequent upon the deportation both to the staff and students of this school, we find ourselves obliged to express our gravest concern and disappointment that the government should have found it necessary at such a moment, and without giving reasons, to take the action that has been taken.

We would like to express our strong conviction that Miss Clarke has, throughout her stay here, made a contribution of real value to the education of children in this country, and would have continued to do so had she been allowed to remain here.

Yours faithfully,

K.M. Smith	K. Ndlovu	W. Masola
P. Symes	N. T. O. Nhlapo	M. Austin
P. Ndlovu	P. J. Ackroyd	J. M. Gatehouse

APPENDIX ONE

Peter Mackay and the role of White Activists in the Nationalist Struggle in Malawi and Zimbabwe

By John McCracken, Honorary Senior Research Fellow at Stirling University.

Peter Mackay, who died aged 87 in 2013, remains largely unknown to both Africanists and Africans under the age of 65. His last years were spent in obscurity in the small Zimbabwean town, Marondera, where he lived alone. Yet, as Terence Ranger, one of the most influential African historians of the last fifty years, has written, Mackay was perhaps the most important, if least recognised, of the disparate band of white activists who involved themselves in nationalist struggles in Central Africa from the 1950s to the 1980s.

Peter John Sutherland Mackay was born in 1926 into a Scottish upper-middle-class family with distinctly imperial connections. Peter himself became head boy at Stowe public school in England, before joining the Scots Guards in 1944. Thriving in the military environment, by 1947 he was serving as senior instructor in the Small Arms Unit at Shrivenham, which is today the Defence Academy of the United Kingdom. It was in this role that Mackay trained several individuals who subsequently became senior officers in the Rhodesian Army.

In 1948 Mackay left the British army, and emigrated to Southern Rhodesia as a trainee tobacco farmer. But while most whites rejoiced in the comforts that came from living in a highly privileged, because racially divided, society, Mackay became increasingly appalled by the combination of materialism and racism that confronted him. Abandoning farming, he turned to journalism in Salisbury (now Harare), and in 1953 joined the multiracial Capricorn Society, becoming its main organising secretary in Central Africa.

In later years, 'Capricorn' became a term of abuse, synonymous with 'sell-out', among Central African nationalists. Today we can recognise that there were merits to be found in a movement distrustful of all nationalisms, white South African as well as black, and dedicated to the erosion of race barriers. But, over time, Mackay came to see, that for all the good intentions of its founders, Capricorn was little more than a front aimed at neutralising African political aspirations. Yet, if Capricorn had proved a blind alley, it had provided Mackay with contacts, quickly transferred into firm friendships, with a number of equally disillusioned African members, among them Leopold Takawira and Herbert Chitepo, who would become prominent leaders of nationalism in Rhodesia.

In his fascinating memoirs, *We Have Tomorrow*, published in 2008, Peter Mackay depicts himself *as* a 'man apart', a highly competent organiser but also someone with a deep desire for privacy. While some white activists were happy to take the limelight, Mackay followed a deliberately more low-key path.

Drawn into nationalist politics in 1959, at the time of the declaration of states of emergency in both Nyasaland and Rhodesia, his first task was to provide practical support for the hundreds of Malawian detainees held without trial at Khami, Gwelo (now Gweru) and Marandellas (now Marondera) prisons in Southern Rhodesia. He then moved to Likhabula, in the shadow of Malawi's Mulanje Mountain, from where he launched a very successful pro-nationalist journal *Tsopano*, at a time when virtually all other outlets of nationalist opinion had been suppressed.

With the foundation of the Malawi Congress Party, Mackay joined the 20 year old Aleke Banda, former Inyathi School student[141] and later Dr Banda's right-hand man, in purchasing a second hand press on which the first copies of the MCP's *Malawi News* were printed. Later he was to ferry Land Rovers, the gift of Kwame Nkrumah of Ghana, from Salisbury to Blantyre. Later still, Mackay wrote the text and took the photographs for the ostensibly authorless *Portrait of Malawi,* a strikingly thoughtful book, the first discussing Malawi's history from an African perspective.

Other white sympathisers tended to focus their activities on a single territory. But, although Peter Mackay came to love Malawi, he was equally concerned with the much more problematic future of Southern Rhodesia. Once again, his involvement in nationalism started with the support he provided for detainees. But in July 1960, for the first and last time, he emerged from the shadows to take a prominent role in organising and leading a great protest march from the township Highfields to the centre of Salisbury following the arrest of the leaders of the National Democratic Party. While this march confirmed in Mackay his total commitment to African nationalism, it also convinced him that it was Africans who must lead the way.

Thereafter, so he claimed, he became a foot-soldier, gladly working under African leadership although, in practice, he could not altogether escape publicity. In 1962 he founded a new anti-colonial

---

[141] See chapter on Aleke Banda, generously provided by John McCracken.

paper, *Chapupu,* only for it to be banned after a few issues by the Rhodesian authorities. The next year he was brought to court for keeping a set of copies of the paper. While the case proceeded, he was arrested and convicted of a further charge: that he had refused to register for military service. His account of the six months he spent in Salisbury gaol is one of the highlights of his memoirs.

Out of prison, with no job and with further charges mounting up against him, Mackay reluctantly took what he saw as the only course available to him, that of breaking his bail and moving to Northern Rhodesia/Zambia, then on the cusp of independence.

With the move to Lusaka, Peter entered a new and dangerous phase in his nationalist activities. His initial job was as organiser of the newly created International Refugee Council for Zambia. This involved the establishment of a transit centre near Lusaka and a farm settlement scheme in the north-east of the country. This centre would provide support for the growing number of Southern African refugees who moved to Zambia, usually in transit to countries further north.

By 1964, Peter had taken on a new responsibility: ferrying refugees by Land Rover on the 900 mile 'freedom road', a largely trackless route extending all the way from Francistown in the Bechuanaland Protectorate (from October 1966, Botswana) to Lusaka. The paths of Mackay and Inyathi School former student J Zwelibanzi Mzilethi intersected at this time.[142]

Peter Mackay's account of his adventures on this route are among the most entertaining in his book. Added to the hazards provided by deep sand and fierce corrugations were dangers that came from

---

[142] See chapter on J.Z. Mzilethi

marauding elephants, prowling lions, poisonous snakes, frequent punctures and the occasional fire enveloping the petrol tank: all of these he succeeded in overcoming. Perceived by some acquaintances as a romantic, he was also a highly practical individual, capable of stripping down an engine when that was required.

From 1965, the dangers facing him increased. In November Ian Smith, the Rhodesian Prime Minister made his Unilateral Declaration of Independence from Britain, asserting that white-controlled Rhodesia was now an independent state. By this time, the two main African parties, the Zimbabwe African People's Union (ZAPU) and the Zimbabwe African National Union (ZANU) were preparing for armed confrontation. As a loyal supporter of ZAPU and its two main leaders in exile, James Chikerema and George Nyandoro, Mackay was faced by the dilemma as to what actions he was prepared to take in the struggle for liberation.

His response was typically idiosyncratic. On the one hand, he equipped himself with a Union Jack which he now carried in his Land Rover, as evidence of his continuing allegiance to a crown and country that Ian Smith and the Rhodesian Front had betrayed. On the other hand, Mackay committed himself, in breach of the agreements that he had made with Botswana government officials, to carrying military equipment for use by ZAPU guerrillas. Over the next year he made several expeditions, carrying military hardware, liaising with guerrillas, always in danger from Rhodesian Special Forces.

There are many features in Mackay's later career that remain obscure. By the late 1960s, he had taken employment in Tanzania on the project to establish a new capital at Dodoma. In 1969 he returned to Zambia, where he became the highly successful representative of the local branch of the Oxford University Press, a role in which he commissioned a number of valuable works on Zambian history. All this time, however, he retained his allegiance to ZAPU, carrying out whatever tasks Chikerema and Nyandoro required of him.

A growing problem was that, with the evolution of nationalist politics, Chikerema and Nyandoro lost power in ZAPU at much the same time as ZANU, soon to be led by Robert Mugabe, took the initiative in penetrating Rhodesia from the east. Peter Mackay had a brief and unhappy time in London working for a pressure group, 'Justice for Rhodesia'. He had an even unhappier time when he followed Chikerema and Nyandoro back to Rhodesia during the so-called Internal Settlement, under which Bishop Muzorewa established a temporary alliance with Smith. The Lancaster House Agreement of December 1979 and Mugabe's decisive election victory in 1980 thus came to Peter as a great relief, even though the party with which he had been most closely involved had been defeated.

For more than 20 years, Peter Mackay had involved himself in the struggle for African political liberation. Along the way he had witnessed many personal tragedies and had experienced many disappointments: the death in prison of his dear friend Leopold Takawira; the tragic death by drowning in Malawi of one of the brightest of all young Zimbabwean intellectuals, Sketchley Samkange; the death in a car accident (or **was** it an accident?) of Dunduza Chisiza, the one Malawian politician who, intellectually, was more than a match for Dr Banda. Most cruel of all, Mackay had witnessed with anguish the deep split that emerged between Banda and his younger Malawian colleagues.

Yet, it is, I think, a precious feature of Mackay that, for all the sense of disillusionment, of anger that he must have felt at times, his deepest concern remained for African liberation, no longer political liberation, but rather liberation from grinding poverty for the poorest and most dispossessed people. Writing an obituary of Peter, Trevor Grundy records that, after 1980, Peter 'saw former colleagues climb greasy poles that led to personal wealth and political corruption'. It is straining credibility that Mackay would have wished to follow their example. But what he did do is all the more remarkable. Terence Ranger in his introduction to *We Have Tomorrow* gives the best account:

> *Someone told (Mackay) that in the north, on the shore of Lake Kariba in the district of Omay, people were starving and eating grass to survive. He drove his yellow Land-Rover up almost impassable roads to Omay; found that the report was true; and thereafter devoted himself to the district. He camped out at the District Administrator's office, high on a bluff overlooking the lake, visited by friendly elephants. He brought in Save the Children and the Cambridge Female Education Trust (CAMFED), which started its support for African secondary school girl pupils in Omay. He built a large 'traditional' hut as a crafts shop for local produce close to the big tourist hotel.*

Mackay set up schools, projects for the blind, clinics and agricultural settlements. And when, after 20 years, aged over 70, he eventually had to withdraw from day to day involvement, he ensured that the Omay Trust would continue, as it does today.

I suggested in my introduction that Mackay was possibly the most important of the white radicals involved in central Africa's nationalist movement. One aspect was his readiness, for better or worse, to involve himself in violence. A second aspect was the unflinching commitment to African liberation that he demonstrated over 40 years. The later careers of most white sympathisers with African nationalism were in relative academic comfort. But this was a far cry from Peter Mackay's long involvement with Omay, or indeed from his final, solitary, poverty-stricken years spent tending a garden at his modest bungalow in Marondera.

What are we to make of Peter Mackay? His uncle Walter described him to me as 'the black sheep of the family.' I imagine that Peter would have enjoyed the title. Rhodesian Front ministers asserted that he was a KGB agent, a claim rejected by Chikerema who informed the Transitional Government, of which he was a part, that Mackay, while working under his direction, 'had undoubtedly made contact with Communist elements' but that 'he had never any genuine association with communist aims'. By contrast, it has recently been suggested to me that, during the early years of the 'Freedom Road', Peter Mackay may have been working with MI6 (the British Secret Service), which at that time had a significant presence in the Bechuanaland Protectorate.

Much of this can only be speculation. But two, apparently contradictory points can be made, each of them leading to the same conclusion: the one that Peter was an exceptionally stubborn, independent-minded person when issues of principle were involved. He acted time and again on what he believed to be right. The second point is that he was steadfast*ly* loyal to those who won his trust.

'We have tomorrow' is a line from a poem by Langston Hughes, quoted by Yatuta Chisiza in 1964 in his last speech in the Malawian parliament before Independence: 'We have tomorrow bright before us like a flame'. Mackay, more than most, had direct experience of the bear pit that could be the nationalist arena. But in choosing this line, more than 40 years later, as the title for his book, he was making a valuable statement. For all its shortcomings, so Ranger wrote, 'African nationalism was once a heroic enterprise for which brave and idealistic people were prepared to suffer and die.' At its heart was a sense of comradeship, transcending race, class and gender.

In my introduction, I suggested that Peter Mackay was largely unknown. This was once true, but the publication of his memoirs, the appearance of reviews of his book and of the obituaries that appeared after his death in 2013 have all added to a growing interest among scholars. In late 2015 Peter Mackay's papers were given to Stirling University where scholars may consult and learn from them. This archive is a comprehensive record of his life, his involvement in the independence movements, and his charitable work.

Pathisa Nyathi adds: *Peter Mackay assisted many ZPRA cadres infiltrating Rhodesia: Tshinga Dube, David Mongwa "Sharpshoot", Roger Matshimini Ncube and others in 1966 when they were on a reconnaissance mission preparing for the Wankie campaign of 1967. Mackay assisted Moffat Hadebe (ex Inyathi School student) when he escaped from Grey Prison into Bechuanaland in 1965. This was after Hadebe and a group of five attacked Zidube Ranch, marking the first shots fired in the Liberation Struggle.*

A record of thanks to Peter Mackay from Walter Mthimkhulu, leader of the March 11th Movement. (See Walter's chapter):

"Peter Mackay's house in Lusaka was the headquarters of the March 11th Movement. If it had not been for Peter Mackay, we'd still be in jail." Walter Mthimkhulu to Marieke Clarke by telephone, 25.03.2018

John McCracken gave a fuller version of this talk at the event held at Stirling University Library to mark the donation of the archives. With John McCracken's permission, Marieke Clarke adapted and edited the paper so it could be used in this book. See in particular chapters about Joshua Mahlathini Mpofu and Walter Mthimkhulu.

John McCracken died while this book was being prepared.

Thanks to academics, mapmakers and artists:
Llyr Pierce designed the map of Zambia and the diagram in Walter Mthimkhulu's chapter. The Bodleian Library advised us.

The map of Matabeleland before Conquest is from the doctoral thesis of Julian Cobbing "The Ndebele under the Khumalos". Lancaster University, 1976.

APPENDIX TWO

OUTLINE HISTORY OF WESTERN-STYLE EDUCATION AT INYATHI MISSION

1859: Robert Moffat, invited by King Mzilikazi, establishes a mission station.
1861: Mrs Annie Thomas is teaching 30 pupils in her home.
1865: A day school for children is started.
Late 1867: Education classes for adults are started.
1882: There is a daily school at Inyathi.
1888: Bowen Rees and Mathambo Ndlovu start a night school.
1898: Mathambo Ndlovu starts a school on an outstation, probably in the Shangani Reserve.
1903: A later Bowen Rees report says there were four schools linked to Inyathi Mission.
1905: Rees reports that there are over 1000 children in schools linked to Inyathi Mission.
1909: Queen Lozikeyi Dlodlo and Prince Tshakalisa Khumalo ask Rees to open new schools.
1913: Bowen Rees reports that there are 13 schools linked to Inyathi Mission and over 500 children attend daily.
1914: Rees reports that 47 children attend the day school at Chief Dakamela's settlement; 80 children attend the night school at Chief Sikhobokhobo's settlement. Prince Tshakalisa Khumalo sends his son Prince Dabulamanzi to school at Inyathi.
1921: Boys' boarding school opens at Inyathi. Inyathi becomes a boys' Industrial Institute.
1929: Teacher training department founded at Inyathi
1938: Teacher training department transferred to Hope Fountain. Inyathi becomes a Central Primary School.
1953: Secondary school for boys opened at Inyathi. Peter Sivalo Mahlangu is the first staff member appointed
1957: Girls admitted to Inyathi secondary school, Carpentry department moved to Hope Fountain.

BOOKS YOU MAY LIKE TO REFER TO:

"These Vessels: the story of Inyati 1859-1959," by Iris Clinton, published Stuart Manning, Bulawayo, 1959. An official LMS history for the centenary of the Mission's founding.

"Education and the London Missionary Society in Matabeleland", by D.G.H. Flood, (M.Ed thesis, University of Bristol, 1974).

"My life in the struggle for the Liberation of Zimbabwe," by Joshua Mahlathini Mpofu (Authorhouse UK Ltd, USA 2014). The story of a freedom fighter who was a student at Inyathi School.

"Lozikeyi Dlodlo, Queen of the Ndebele: 'A very dangerous and intriguing woman' " by Marieke Faber Clarke with Pathisa Nyathi (Amagugu Publishers, Bulawayo, 2010). History of Matabeleland up to 1918. Third edition published 2017 with new material.

"Rev. Bowen Rees: a missionary for Matabeleland" by Marieke Clarke with Pathisa Nyathi (Amagugu Publishers, Bulawayo, 2017). A distinguished early LMS missionary who knew and deeply cared for King Lobhengula.

"Welshman Hadane Mabhena: A voice for Matabeleland," by Marieke Clarke with Pathisa Nyathi (Amagugu Publishers, Bulawayo, 2016)

"The Mambo Hills: historical and religious significance" by Marieke Clarke (AmaBooks, Bulawayo, 2008). Background to the childhood of some of our contributors.

"The Lusaka Years: the ANC in Exile in Zambia" by Hugh Macmillan, (Jacana Media, South Africa, 2013) Background to the Zimbabwe Liberation War.

www.ingramcontent.com/pod-product-compliance
Lightning Source LLC
Chambersburg PA
CBHW050533300426
44113CB00012B/2076